THOMAS WOLFE AS I KNEW HIM

and Other Essays

THOMAS WOLFE

AS I KNEW HIM

and other essays

VARDIS FISHER

Alan Swallow, *Denver*

For the
        Ellis Foote
lost
somewhere high on the mountain
mist-enfolded cloud-scarfed
demon-crossed
his soul in the last moment visible
orphan-faced storm-wharfed

Note

The author deplores as much as any reader possibly can repetitions of the Wolfe, chapter-four material and the Sammy-Eugene-Vridar theme and hopes the reader will bear in mind that these appeared in essays or talks in different years and places. They are so germane to the author's point of view that it has been thought that to delete them would weaken the arguments which they support.

Contents

An Unforgettable Character

I first saw the strange out-of-this-world man at one of the huge Sunday gatherings in Chicago's Washington Park, which were known locally as the Bug Club. It was the summer of 1923. I was standing in the outer fringe of several hundred persons, listening to an intense, impassioned, long-haired soap-boxer, who was demolishing the American free enterprise system corporation by corporation, when, glancing round at the faces, my gaze met a pair of soft, eager, childlike eyes in a bearded and horribly emaciated face.

He was tall, extremely tall—all of six feet four or five, I would say; and so fleshless and cadaverous that he was little more than a reedlike skeleton in filthy rags. And he was lonely—I sensed it at once—one of the loneliest men I was ever to know.

I smiled and at once he answered with a smile, and came shuffling over to me—for he had no walk, only a loose, twitching, long-legged shuffle. He came over, eager but humble, like one who had been kicked ten times for every time he had been smiled at; like a homeless dog

---

*Invited by the editors of *The Reader's Digest* to submit an essay on an unforgettable character I foolishly sent this. The horrified editors returned it in a fumigated envelope.

9

ready to be friendly but ready to retreat, his smile showing a mouthful of hideously decayed teeth, and his soul.

His appearance was utterly unwashed and filthy and I think you could have smelled him a hundred feet away when there was no breeze. I was to learn later that he was homeless, friendless, a social outcast; a man who never labored for his keep but ate what was handed to him at the back doors of cafes, or did not eat, days on end; who wore such castoff rags as he could pick up—his trousers that day were so short that the bottoms of the legs were about halfway between ankles and knees, revealing hairy unwashed shins; and his shoes, so worn out they were falling apart, were held together with ordinary store twine and were several sizes too big for his feet. That is one reason why he shuffled. If he had lifted his feet the shoes would have fallen off. He stuttered horribly when he tried to speak but I was to observe later that when he addressed an audience on the only subject dear to his heart he did not stutter at all.

I thought of him first as an odorous phantom. I did not know then what a personality lived in the skin and bones over which the rags were hung.

I knew him for more than a year as Bowles or Boles—I never knew whether this was his first or last name, or how he spelled it. I never asked. For such a person the name seemed not to matter at all. I never learned whether he had people or was completely alone in life; where he was born and what his early life had been like; and whether he had ever married. After realizing what fires burned in his fleshless breast I never thought of him in terms of birth, family, friends. Has anyone ever wondered who St. Anthony's mother was?—or Isaiah's or John's?

He had had almost no formal education—I think he had never finished grammar school—but somehow, in such libraries as would admit him, he had schooled himself. He had mastered, at least well enough to read the original documents, Latin, ancient Greek, Hebrew, and he had a smattering of other languages, such as Syriac and Aramaic. His great passion was theology, the Testaments, his gospel; he had got so much of the Testaments by heart that I never ceased being astonished. He could quote from either for hours on end and it was a memorable experience to see his face, indeed, his whole being, light up when his deep voice uttered the more majestic verses from Isaiah, Job, Matthew, or Paul. It was then that I knew that I was in the presence of a remarkable man.

When I first met him he was eaten alive by doubts—doubts about certain Catholic dogmas and doctrines. I never clearly understood what they were, or much cared. They turned on various translations, which he questioned; on fine points in exegesis; and though after we became friends he talked to me about them many times, his face and manner so intense that listening to him was painful, I never quite made out the nature of the doubts that tormented him.

One thing I did clearly perceive, that he was trying to return to the simple way of life of the traditional Galilean. He *had* returned. Nowhere have I ever known a man one-half so Jesuslike—and I mean the Jesus represented by the Gospels. Boles had literally accepted certain teachings: he had gone forth without purse or scrip to bear the glad news; he lived from hand to mouth, unwashed, in rags. What did the early Fathers say about Jesus? Cyril said he was mean of aspect, "even beyond the ordinary race of men"; Irenaeus characterized him as infirmus, ingloriosus and indecorus; Tertullian, Justin, and Hippolytus said he looked like a slave; and Bishop Eusebius, the early Church historian, wrote that "a razor never came upon his head, he never anointed with oil, and never used a bath." Boles lived in rags and filth, as the Church Fathers said Jesus had lived. He slept where he could—under a tree in the park, if policemen would let him do it; or, in colder weather, on the floor of a cafe or in a garage or cellar.

He was dedicated to a message of love. Utterly without guile, so far as I could tell, or meanness; without envy or malice; without a sense of caring for his body, much less a sense of property, this gentle man was ready to teach anyone who would listen. At the Sunday afternoon gatherings, which in fair weather were large, or at the weekday evening gatherings, which were smaller, he preached his gospel, usually to only a handful of persons; and these invariably included cynics and scoffers, who strove to interrupt, confuse, and torment him. The demagogs and windbags drew large audiences. I never saw Boles with more than twenty, save once, when he disputed with a Mormon missionary.

* * *

11

The wife of a former friend, who was a college professor, once told me that when he was introduced to her his first words were, "Do you believe in God?" On being assured that she did not he felt bewitched, and wooed her within the frame of Karl Marx. Boles asked a woman the same question, and on being told that she did he wooed her within the frame of the Old and New Testaments.

Among the people who came to these gatherings was a short, stooped, middle-aged, and very homely woman. She had a cast in one eye or was blind; her whole face was distorted and misshapen. I talked to her and learned that she was a graduate of an excellent university and had a fine mind. It occurred to me that this strange man and this strange woman might have things in common — that they might fall in love, or in any case become companions. And so it was that I introduced them.

On learning that she believed in God Boles felt that his first task was to persuade her to his view of religion; and this he accomplished in record time, or she allowed him to believe that he had; and it was not until then that I saw him sometimes looking at her as a man in love looks at a woman. In the evenings now and then they would sit apart from the crowds, clasping hands, and now and then looking into the eyes of one another and smiling. It was a love affair that seemed to me to have a great deal of beauty and tenderness in it, but whether they ever married I was never to know. They were always together when I saw them, and when Boles addressed a group she would stand close by him, and once in a while he would interrupt the flow of his learning and eloquence to look down at her and answer her smile of encouragement and approval. She cleaned him up and got him some better clothes but she never persuaded him to have his long graying hair shingled. It still fell down his neck to his shoulders.

* * *

For me the most incredible and memorable part of my association with this man lay in the fact that he actually founded a church, or sect or splinter faith, of his own. I was a witness to its inception and growth. For me it was a fascinating psychological study, not only of Boles himself but of some of the persons whom he converted to his point of view. A few of them were not by any means emotional

12

or intellectual illiterates. Among them, I remember, were a dentist, a lawyer, and a business man who dressed lavishly, affected a walking-stick, and wore a diamond as large as a bean. It would be easy to believe that his disciples were playing Boles for the fool, and it is true that in his group there were always a few callow scoffers who twitted and mocked him. It was characteristic of the man that he never looked with anger or pity on those who tried to hold him up to ridicule. There were scoffers, yes, but most of them seemed to be sincere, and in the group was about a hundred persons when I saw Boles the last time. His followers brought food and clothes to him, and he looked quite clean and handsome after he became their priest.

When he had accomplished a faithful group of his own—this was in the summer of 1924 — he expounded difficult points of doctrine to them, for he was at heart an exegete rather than a prophet. He enjoyed nuances and subtleties in meanings, and it occurred to me that he really belonged back in the Middle Ages, possibly at the knee of Aquinas, when hairsplitting engaged the minds and consumed the passions of men.

His arguments invariably rested upon mistranslations of the holy word; I was unable at the time to tell if he was right or wrong but I took a few notes. Since then I have become familiar with much of the greatest scholarship on the Testaments, and in every instance where I have checked him this remarkable man was right.

He once gave an entire lesson to Matthew, I, 23, saying that the word translated virgin did not mean virgin at all (you can imagine with what avidity I made a note of *that*, in that summer). Salomon Reinach in his *Orpheus* tells us that as early as the second century "the Jews perceived the error and pointed it out to the Greeks" — meaning the Greek Christians; and I find in St. Jerome (Adv. Juv, 1,32): "I know that the Jews are accustomed to meet us with the objection that in Hebrew the word *Almah* does not mean a *virgin*, but a *young woman*. And, to speak truth, a virgin is properly called *Bethulah*" — which is what Boles told us. The error goes back to an early and faulty translation of *Isaiah*, 7, 14, "Therefore the Lord himself shall give you a sign; Behold, a virgin shall conceive, and bear a son, and shall call his name Immanuel." In the Hebrew Bible it reads, "the young woman shall conceive . . ." The Isaiah prophecy meant only that a woman would have a son who would be king of Israel, but the Christians had to have a virgin because it was a tradition that superhuman heroes were born of virgins.

The number of mistranslations in any copy of the Testaments is large. Among those which Boles pointed out, besides the above, of which I made note, are these. He said the word Babel (bab-el) meant literally the gate of God — and so it does. He dwelt in learned detail on the words, Our Father which art in heaven, saying that they had been misunderstood. Of these words Professor Enslin (*Christian Beginnings*, 102) says that they were not "as has often been popularly supposed, an indication of a radical about face from the conception of God held by orthodox Judaism, but was one of the many legacies of the Synagogue to the Church. Nor is it to be argued that while for Judaism God may have been the Father of the nation, it remained for Christianity to personalize the relationship, to make him the Father of the individual."

Boles told us that the words in *Hosea, 6, 5*, meant, not "thy judgments are as the light that goeth forth" but "My judgment is as the light that goes forth" — and I find this confirmed in Professor Bewer's *The Literature of the Old Testament*, 431. Boles said the translation should not be Shew-bread but Presence-bread — and Professor Duff (*Religion of Judaism*, 76) supports him. Boles said that the Hebrew word *Goim* did not mean heathen; and Duff says (247) that this translation "is a mistake inherited from the Greek language with its word Ethnos, which is not a religiously condemnatory word at all."

I became so curious about this man and his passion that I began to read in the scholarship on the Testaments, and make notes, on my reading and on what Boles said. If any reader is as curious as I was he can do no better, I think, than to begin with Max J. Margolis' excellent little volume, *The Story of Bible Translations*.

I shall lift two or three other instances from my notes, observing first what Schurer says in the fifth volume of his great work, that the Jews "often reproached the Christians with their ignorance of the genuine text of Scripture" and that the text of the Septuagint "has come down to us solely by the tradition of the Christian Church," with all the "base corruption of the text." It was this significant fact which Boles had discovered in the library at the University of Chicago. He said there was no authority to support the notion that Moses and his followers came to the Red Sea. Oesterley and Robinson (*Hebrew Religion*, 138) say: "The fact must be recognized that there is no authority for bringing the Red Sea into the narrative. The Old Testament speaks of Yam-Suph as the waters in which the Egyptians were overwhelmed; that means either the 'Reed Sea' or more correctly the 'Sea of Weeds.' " Boles said the translation "a mercy-seat" was wrong, and Duff says this translation is not only "thoroughly mistaken" but has "led to mistakes even in Paul's writings, and in the long succession of theological theories throughout history." Boles told us that the word *Jehovah* should not be used for God, that the proper word was *Yahweh*. All the Higher Critics say that this is so.

It would be folly to labor the matter, but let us glance briefly at the *Catholic Encyclopedia*: "The Church had adopted the Septuagint as its own; this differed from the Hebrew not only by the addition of several books and passages but also by innumerable variations of text, due partly to the ordinary process of corruption in the transcription of ancient books, partly to the culpable temerity, as Origen called it, of correctors who used not a little freedom in making 'corrections,' additions, and suppressions, partly to mistakes in translation, and finally in great part to the fact that the original Septuagint had been made from a Hebrew text quite different from that fixed at Jamnia as the one standard by the Jewish Rabbis."

Boles had got on the trail of all this and was as eager as a hunting dog on a scent. He was forced to conclude that the Church in essential matters had strayed from the original meanings and that a new sect ought to be founded. My interest was not in points of dogma but in this remarkable man and the ease with which he established a new faith — or perhaps we should say a multitude of corrections upon an old faith.

* * *

At that time I was acquiring large French and German vocabularies; it was my habit to rise early and walk for an hour or two, memorizing words. One morning late in the summer of 1924 I was passing through the park when, looking round me, I saw a group of people under a large tree. Boles was holding mass for his handful of followers.

When he saw me watching him the incredible fellow dropped everything and came over. He looked down at me, smiling, eager, questioning, humble, and asked, "Huh-huh-how am I duh-duh-doing?" "Wonderful!" I said. "What is your text today?" "Muh-muh-Matthew eighteen and one." The moment he began to recite the verses he ceased stuttering: "At the same time there came disciples unto Jesus, saying, Who is the greatest in the kingdom of heaven? And Jesus called a little child unto him, and set him in the midst of them . . ."

"The shepherd should never leave his sheep," I said. "Go back to your flock."

At once he turned and went back. For a few minutes I observed him, this tall, terribly thin man, acting as priest and religious father to his group. It was a lovely morning, and when, a little later, his flock began to sing I was deeply moved. There came to me another verse from Matthew, "And Jesus saith unto him, The foxes have holes, and the birds of the air have nests; but the son of man hath not where to lay his head."

That was the last time I saw him. I think he must have died long ago, for he looked sick and frail, with deep lines of want and fatigue in his face. His "church," I have no doubt, perished with him, but far more religions have perished on this planet than now survive. I am sure that the spirit of the man still lives, like the morning and the evening, and hope in the souls of men; and wherever he may be I like to think that his most fitting epitaph is these words from *First Corinthians*, whose noble meaning first came to me from the tall man at the Bug Club:

> Every man's work shall be made manifest: for the day shall declare it, because it shall be revealed by fire; and the fire shall try every man's work of what sort it is.

Profanity in Fiction

In American literary criticism of the moment there is, it seems to me, an ironic paradox. No more than a cursory reading of reviews discovers two statements, repeated over and over and sometimes with angry emphasis. One says a novel is not convincing, it is unreal, its characters are made of straw and its events of Christmas tinsel; and the other says that characters are brutish and brutal and depraved, details are loathsome, and the speech of the people is obscene, profane, and disgusting. Novels can, of course, portray life and still be inoffensive to the pure in heart, but in such instances the nose-blowing and swearing are probably omitted, for even preachers now and then blow up in soul-cleansing rages, and virgins have functions that the censors pretend not to know about. I'd suspect that a novel which comes forth with the imprimatur of a girls' boarding school has a lot of unwritten chapters.

The truth, as I make it out, is that some critics demand only certain kinds of realism, conventional, germless, and thrice blessed. They are dismayed by what Cabell has called the *demiurge;* they are determined to find, not man as he is but man as they think they

*Published about 1929 in a journal whose name I have forgotten.

would have set him down in the Garden. They love euphemisms, even on the tongues of brigands and scoundrels; and they want to read about only those things which they feel go into the making of a noble nation and a pure marriage. The dynamic illusions must operate toward ends which incorporate and are founded upon the carefully nourished myth of what man ought to be.

As a result of this attitude which pervades and fumigates those who choose the Pulitzer masterpieces we have a fiction which only in rare instances touches life. Its method, Ludwig Lewisohn says, "is either frankly medieval, illustrating in temper the result of a preconceived system of moral categories; or else it is written in the service of that smug and hollow moral perfectionism which is the most unpleasant quality of the 18th century. The first of these two methods is found in nearly all popular fiction and plays and would be negligible if it did not enjoy, as it does in no other country in the world, the patronage of the formally educated." Mr. Lewisohn is pretty rough on the word *educated*; he meant no doubt those who emerge from our school system with what is jokingly called a bachelor's degree in the arts.

Most Americans demand fiction that ministers to their infantile fantasies. I have no objection to that kind, for I doubt that any man knows what is best for those on lower levels of culture and taste. None of us has the right to take from our more stupid and ignorant brethren those joys that make them feel momentarily wise or illustrious — and least of all in a democracy which is driven by its quaint notions of equality to pull the bottom levels up and the top levels down. Most of us live pretty mean and cabined lives, not once in ten years or fifty touching real adventure or glory; and it may be that the infantile fantasies save a lot of people from madness. It gets us nothing to scorn the artistic standards of the mass: those standards were once ours, somewhere back in the past, and those which we cherish today may conceivably become theirs, somewhere in the future.

What irks me is those persons who think they have the knowledge and taste to determine not only what people should read but what authors should write. Just out of Yale or Princeton with a bachelor's degree they fancy themselves as literary critics. Either they don't know the past or are unable to learn its lessons; otherwise the almost total neglect of such authors as Stendhal and Melville and the praise and honors poured upon hacks, long since forgotten, would force them to wonder if possibly there are two or three things in the world they haven't yet mastered. Stendhal, for instance, was in his lifetime rejected and is now acclaimed for precisely those virtues which most American book reviewers would chase out of house and home.

And yet they go on, month after month, condemning one book because it is unreal, and another because it is too real. In regard to one novel they lament its deficiencies in local color, colloquial speech, and blood and marrow in the characters; but another they pitch into the fireplace or send out with the garbage because it has those virtues which only a week ago they were begging for. What they should do is draw a list of those things in human motives and behavior which make them feel ill, and the existence of which they choose not to recognize, except in the Calibans groveling in the mire. They should make it plain to their readers that arson and theft and murder are perfectly moral things to write about, but that lust and profanity are out of bounds. Unless they have been so successful in repressing the unpleasant that their wits are completely addled they should face up with an English critic to the fact that the person in whose thoughts if not in whose speech profanity is never present is a monster whom we all wish never to see.

Most American book reviewers seem to think that literary art is a eunuch. Not one of these self-established guardians of public morality would, Heywood Broun says, admit that an immoral book or even the vilest pornography could have the slightest influence on them. When they come in contact with such things they are like globules of purest quicksilver going through an intestinal tract. It is always the other fellow, John Doe or Susan Jones, who is in danger of filling his cranium with filth and setting up as the teacher of small boys. They have no capacity to learn that pornography is not in the symbols called words but in the nasty minds of those who at every opportunity shout hosannahs to decency. It is a commonplace fact of life that the one who suffers fevers and chills over an obscenity is also the one with the most avid and insatiable interest in what happens behind drawn shades and whose scrawny emotional life finds sly midnight paths to the expurgated passages.

There is what a writer has called the "secret terrorism" that falls in a sinister shadow over much book reviewing but like small pox and typhoid it will pass. These Comstocks may some day learn that the bedroom can teach us much more than the drawing room, and has in it more drama and probably more beauty. There are those today who tell us that we are on a sickbed of culture and we may be, but I have personally known a few prophets of social collapse and chaos and have found them all touched by the messianic myth. We do have acid-stained barbarians and intrusive minions and traitorous Brahmins. And we have the Philistines who make the writing of books unpleasant for those who try to write honest books. I find none of them more depressing and unnecessary than those who think book characters depraved if they cuss a blue streak. Let's look at the psychology of that.

I was reared on a frontier in the far west, where the only people I knew and the only people in that land were crude uncouth folk, without graces of any sort, but with the traditional reverence for Church and God. Most of the men and some of the women were hard talkers and hard actors. Swinburne, famous for his fund of invective, would have been abashed and silenced if he had heard some of the frontiersmen when they smashed a thumb with a hammer or stumbled over a hidden root and paralyzed a kneecap. These men were less vicious, I think, than those who keep themselves pure with heck and gee-whiz, one a euphemism for hell and the other for Jesus. I lived with such men from childhood up and I learned their vocabularies, and on occasion I cursed until I almost fainted or dropped dead from depletion. It's a wonderful piece of therapy and catharsis if you know how to do it; but it's no good at all if while invoking divine wrath on your enemies you feel that God is looking in the window and your mother is fetching the chokecherry stick.

I was told by my mother and other pious folk that swearing was wrong but nobody told me why; I never related it to God or religion or to any of the other concepts which restrain in some people the impulses to rape and murder. Nor did my father and the other men.

20

When they felt a need to curse a blue streak they did it because they had done it from early childhood. When they used the word *god* as an oath it was in no way associated in their minds with the divine being who called forth their prayers on Sunday. God and Jesus and Christ and Holy Ghost were all as meaningless, when used profanely, as Moses and Abraham and Jacob. They were a part of the furious stock-in-speech with which men loosed their furies and asserted their manhood.

The commonest term of abuse familiar to me as a child and a favorite with all men had to do with the dog family. I still don't know why the female dog is such a vile creature that her son is about the lowest thing a man in a rage can think of. This troubled me in adolescence; I wondered why the son of a bitch was so much more offensive than the son of a cow or a mare — and all the more because the dog seemed to me to be the favorite of all human pets and of all animals the most loved. I have seen men turn red and clench their fists when called a son of a bitch, whereas if they had been called the son of a moose they would have thought it a joke. Use the term *son of a bitch* in a novel and reviewers shudder and turn to Roget to find the proper words to characterize you. Use such terms as son of a cheetah or son of a doe and they might think you have a sense of humor.

I wouldn't know what the hypersensitive think of Max Eastman's shrewd remark that profanity and poetry are of the same mother, or of my own feeling that there is more rosy passion and stainless beauty in an outburst of sincere and picturesque profanity than in a bale of the dithyrambic nonsense which is interred every week or month in our magazines. In any case the chronic use of expurgated words is in no way different from chronic use of their euphemisms, such as golly and gosh; the former are just as meaningless to those who use them, and like the latter merely serve as safety valves to let off the bottled up frustrations and repressions and hates. People accustomed to oaths pay no more attention to them than people accustomed to prayer pay to it. Both are harmless and delightful habits and are offensive only to those whose habits are of a different nature.

I would go so far as to say that the habit of profanity is a useful and perhaps necessary agent in the promotion of temperance and sanity. We'd need a lot more psychiatrists and lunatic wards without it. It cleanses the emotional system and scatters down the winds those anxieties and furies which people sit on, until some day they are blown over the moon, or that corrode the inner being until it is lined with iron rust. A good uninhibited fit of cussing gives one the same feeling of relief and the inner heavenly calm that sometimes follow prolonged weeping or prayer. And it is a form of prayer, I suppose. In any case it is a magnificent tonic, like any good tonic when not overused; and if, as some say, we are a languid and depleted people on a sickbed of culture, or in a national neurosis or psychosis, I'd think that a long spell of cussing from ocean to ocean might do a good deal to dissipate the spite and venoms, the bottled up thefts and murders and adulteries, and open the national psyche to a blue sky and scented winds.

If I implied a moment ago that the degenerates who say "son of a bitch" are safer to live around and healthier in mind and emotions than the creatures who are wan and weary with pieties and holiness, I meant it. It's a most unrelieved form of ignorance which supposes that civilization (whatever that is) has filtered the ferocity and bestiality out of those sinister souls who send Christmas cards every December and pretend to believe in equality and justice twelve months of the year. The war to make the world safe for democracy showed us that the only difference between us and the apes is that we stink to the high heavens of inhibitions and repressions. The most chaste of us, a wise man has said, have thoughts which, if published, would scandalize the barbers and bell hops. Even Horace, a rather sharp cricket, could write that he's armed without who's innocent within. A more completely false statement was never written and every profaning man knows it. Even Bunyan, that holy of holies, now and then gave himself over to the task of cursing everything under the sun, and then, cleansed and invigorated, returned to the service of his Father.

Some try to restrain the demon and teach him good manners, and some of us let the demon out for an airing. We who are sometimes called degenerate frankly reveal those things which our critics wear themselves out trying to conceal. We say "son of a bitch" and they say "son of a gun" and we both mean the same thing, though they

22

assume that God will give them the benefit of the doubt. It really all comes down to what we are accustomed to; there is even distrust in most people of those who talk in a strange tongue. If in childhood I had heard, when men were angered and frustrated, the cry, "My mother is a whore!" I'd have grown up using it and thinking nothing of it. Or if I had been taught that "son of a gun" was offensive to the Almighty but that "son of a bitch" in no way disturbed him in this essay I'd be trying to put you on friendly terms with "son of a gun."

I look with favor on the person who spouts the poison and poetry out of him and I don't particularly care what words he uses, if they seem to be old friends. Efforts to establish holiness down in the simian depths produced Davidson's nun, the unwashed fanatics immured in stone cells, and the New Jersey preacher who one day in the middle of a sermon fell headlong into a fit of cussing and held his flock entranced and paralyzed for half an hour. I wouldn't want to look into his soul and sniff its odors, and I like to remember that a wasp entered him and for a little while set him free. Most of all I don't want to get on intimate terms with those who pitch my books into fires and call me degenerate merely because I am a past master in a tried and true form of soul-cleansing.

A frank acceptance of reality, George Meredith said, is the only firm basis for the ideal. If fiction is to portray life and not the sterilized and fumigated view of it favored by those sunk in their repressions we had better believe Anatole France when he tells us that human nature is "harsh, egotistical, jealous, sensual, ferocious" and that we preserve and nourish vices when we hide them. So let my critic shed his Sunday school glow, look around him to see if he has any sense of humor at all, and realize that when he turns purple and shouts, "If Fisher says life is like that I am here to tell him it isn't!" he is calling the whole world's attention to those harsh, egotistical, jealous, sensual, ferocious traits which with both hands he is trying to push down in himself and out of sight. What a poor unhappy son of a bitch he is.

Thomas Wolfe as I Knew Him

On learning that I knew Thomas Wolfe, members of his cult — and one runs into them everywhere — invariably ask, "What was he *really* like?" If I give my impression of what he was like, they then ask, "Why don't you write something about him?" I have had in mind doing just that for almost ten years now. This impulse in me has always been strongest when I have read something about him written by another. This is true because Wolfe was a controversial figure and still is. Almost nobody when viewing him has been dispassionate. Mr. Herbert J. Muller, who published a study of Wolfe in 1947, points out that persons see only his "splendid gifts" or his "shocking sins." Like a certain psychologist they see in him the greatest writer of his time; or with Bernard De Voto they cry impatiently that genius is not enough. Or with W. H. Auden they may dismiss his work as so much grandiose rubbish. The blind men are busy with the elephant, but Wolfe was not all trunk or tail or wall. Though I was fond of him and greatly admire some things in his work, I think I can view him without the adulation of his cultists. Though much in

*First published in *Tomorrow,* Apr., 1951, under the editor's title, My Experiences with Thomas Wolfe.

his work I simply cannot stand, I think I need not fall into the contempt and condescension of his severest critics.

Well, we shall see.

I vividly recall the time I first saw him. In the fall of 1928 I joined the English faculty of Washington Square College. About twenty-five or thirty of us occupied one huge room, with desks placed back to back, so that when we sat at our desk we faced a colleague. For some of us four desks were placed in such manner. I sat on the aisle, and Hal White, a poet, was my deskmate on the left. In this room at that time were men — and women — who were later to make names for themselves. A few of them, like Eda Lou Walton, already had names. Among those to be heard from were Frederic Prokosch, Margaret Schlauch, and Edwin Burgum. It was quite a brilliant English faculty and our department head was inordinately proud of it.

One morning, just after the turn of the year, there entered a man who, I observed at once, attracted instant and, in some of his colleagues, critical attention. My back was to the hall doorway and I did not see him when he came in. I did not see him until he strode past me and dropping a pile of books on a desk across the aisle sank sprawling to a chair. He was so huge, his stride was so long and loose, his dark hair so uncombed, his dark eyes so unhappy and suspicious, and his whole bearing so obviously that of one who felt himself called to an uncommon destiny that I stared at him, fascinated. I felt in him then what he had confessed or was to confess in his books and letters: "By God, I have genius and I shall yet force the inescapable fact down the throats of the rats and vermin who wait for the proof." I felt what he was to say, "Giving my brain and my heart to these stupid little fools; talking like an angel or a God in a language too few of them will understand." I sensed in his whole being his conviction: "There are few heroic lives: about the only one I know a great deal about is my own." His manner of saying these things may repel us but we must accept their essential truth.

For a few moments I slyly studied the man. Turning at last to Hal White, I asked in a whisper, "Who is that?" and in a whisper he said, "Tom Wolfe." I had heard the name from our chairman, who had spoken to me about him, saying that at the moment Wolfe was abroad. But I was not prepared for the response of our colleagues. Several of them were also slyly observing Wolfe and in most of the faces I saw unmistakable distaste.

Seated at my desk I faced uptown. Wolfe, sitting across the aisle and two rows up, faced downtown; and so it was that I had a clear view of him when he sat at his desk and I at mine. I covertly studied him — for without realizing it he invited, almost demanded, attention; and I became aware after a little that Wolfe knew that I was observing him. His face and manner showed it. He resented my furtive but persistent scrutiny but never once did he meet my gaze. It was not his way, I was to learn later, to look anyone straight in the eye. In all my hours with him he never held my gaze for more than a moment, and then only to manifest his morbid intolerance of the fixed and searching stare.

He was not often at his desk. It was not his habit, as it was with most of us, to read class papers at the desk, to prepare notes and lectures there and consult with students there. Every time that he came to his desk I perceived that he was restless, impatient, suspicious, eager to be off. He knew that several of us were trying to discover what sort of man he was, and though no doubt he was flattered he showed only contempt. He had prodigious contempt for pedants, even for college teachers; his contempt for those around him was so plain, yet so childlike in its defensive pose, that I was amused and delighted; and every time he came in I watched him and he knew that I watched him. But he never met my eyes and he never said hello. He never, so far as I observed him, said hello to anyone in that office, when he came in. He simply strode in, sprawled at his desk and brooded, his eyes flickering with spite, scorn, contempt, malice, anxiety, fear; and after a few minutes he would rise and go away. But again and again I tricked him. I would pretend to be immersed in reading, when, suddenly looking up, I would surprise him watching me. At once he would look away, the sardonic distaste in his countenance becoming deeper and darker than his own skin.

* * *

Well, I knew, of course, that here was an extraordinary person, an extraordinary child, lonely, lost, obsessed, embittered, in the great

26

hulking form of a man. Before I ever exchanged a word with Wolfe I thought I knew a great deal about him. For I was another child, lonely and lost, and I recognized my kin. I also sensed that Wolfe suspected that I was looking deeper into him than he wanted anyone to look.

It was inevitable that he should have come to me at last. I recall that moment. My first novel* had been published the previous October. Wolfe's first novel had been accepted by Maxwell Perkins while Wolfe was abroad, and was to be pulished this year. He came up to me one day and said briefly and simply, "I read your novel and liked it," and turned away. But he came again and we bacame friends, and during the next couple of years we saw quite a bit of one another.

Wolfe, whose intuitions were sharp and incisive, recognized in me a kindred spirit. Though my childhood had been spent at a lonely frontier outpost, deep in the West, and his in a city in the East, we had many things in common. I had indeed more in common with him than I have had with any other friend. We had in common the kind of childhood that had tortured us and driven us almost to lunacy; the same lonely introversion of spirit; the same fantastically over-developed idealism all tangled up with deep distrust of human motives; the same montrous self-pity; the same fright and anxieties; the same kind of identification with the opposite sex and hatred of father; the same hatred of mother; the same problem with women; the

---

*In *Thomas Wolfe at Washington Square*, New York Univ. Press, 1954, Professor Russell Krauss writes: "Publishing almost simultaneously in the fall of 1929—Fisher's book was the first installment of his *In Tragic Life* tetralogy—the two young authors had, as I recall, exchanged presentation copies of their books . . . . Vardis admitted to me with a rival's grudge that the book had merits . . . he confided his opinion that Wolfe would prove a one-book man . . . . Wolfe expressed to me an almost identical opinion of Vardis and his book. . . ."

I can't imagine how Prof. Krauss got so mixed up. *In Tragic Life* was published more than two years after *Look Homeward, Angel*, and almost a year after I had seen Wolfe for the last time! We never exchanged books. I have no memory of having commented on the Wolfe novel, to Professor Krauss or to anyone else; and if Wolfe made any such comment to him about mine, it could hardly have been just "a few days later"!

27

same contempt for pretentiousness and sham, that came largely from an unhappy recognition of sham in ourselves; the same contempt for most human beings, that was only displaced contempt for self — though this I did not known then and I think Wolfe never learned; the same frenzied desire to prove our worth and leave our name on a page of history, though aware that fame was a bauble, and personal immortality the hope of a ravaged soul; the same gross, offensive, and sometimes insufferable egoism that was less egoism than a defense against our overdeveloped submissive tendencies, which in both of us were very strong; the same naked need of spiritual shelters but scorn of formalized religions; and the same tendency to psychic impotence. We were making the same kind of struggle to come out of childhood darkness, but I had at that time recognized that the "door" was only a deeper darkness.

We had had — our talks together soon revealed this — the same kind of problems with parents and other relatives. Both had had a dominant overzealous mother who, though well-meaning and devoted, had never understood her strange child; and the unhappy relationship with mother had colored with unfortunate results our relations with other women. We had a father who had scared the living daylights out of us, mine with the crude brutalities of the frontier, Wolfe's (these anyway were two) with declamation and fire.

Anyone who would understand Wolfe must understand his relationship with his mother. Mr. Muller, I think, almost entirely missed it. Phallic symbols run through Wolfe's books in teeming numbers, and though Muller alludes to a few of them he apparently did not grasp their significance. In one instance he says that Wolfe's quest of a father "sometimes looks more like the quest of a mother, a yearning for the womb." As though there could be any question about it! He reminds us that Wolfe suckled until he was three and a half years old, and slept with his mother until he was a big boy. In a footnote he suggests that Wolfe got the idea " of the search for a father from Maxwell Perkins rather than Joyce"; and a few pages later speaks of "the progress he has made in his search for a father, a door, a home." Door and home have never been with any people, so far as I know, father-symbols: one wonders what the ancient Semitic "door of life" means to Mr. Muller. Why, he asks, was Wolfe such a cad with "Esther" and gives Wolfe's answer, that he returned to the "demon" in man. The demon idea, Muller says, is not sheer nonsense. It is that and nothing else. Wolfe simply refused to face up to his repressions and went off half-cocked into ancient superstition-symbols. In his early work, Muller points out, Wolfe introduced the theme that he could not go home again, "but by home he means simply Asheville." I don't think his subconscious mind meant that at all. By home he meant his mother and by his mother he meant the door.

Jung puts it this way: "In order not to be conscious of his desire for incest (his regressive impulse toward animal nature) the son lays the entire blame on the mother, whence results the image of the 'dreaded mother.' 'Mother' becomes a specter of anxiety to him." Wolfe's mother, as anyone can learn by reading his letters, became such a specter to Wolfe. His bitter reproaches fill many pages: "You don't know me, Mama. I'm not important to you." Again: "I have not yet ceased hoping or believing that there may be left in some of you some genuine atom of affection, sympathy, and good will for me." Wolfe went to Europe year after year for his own profit and pleasure, spending all of his own money on himself, and in letter after letter, year after year, writing to his hard-working mother for money. She seems to have sent it every time he asked for it. After all, he had slept with her until he was (in her words) "a great big boy. I kept him a baby." After his curls were cut "the sad part to me — my baby was gone — he was getting away from me." In any case he was trying to; that is why he kept running to Europe. That he was never able to get away from her and then return, as the adult returns, was his tragedy. He writes bitterly from Europe that she has forgotten him and will never see him again — and a few days later she is sending him money. His self-pitying and petulant ingratitude to his mother makes pretty painful reading, though we do of course know out of what his ingratitude came.

His father-problem is just as clear. One day I was with him in that enormous bleak ugly room in which he lived for a while, when he did something that astonished me. Scattered over the chairs and floor were books, papers, letters, manscripts, clothes. We had spent two or three hours there when, called back to our duties, we prepared to leave. Wolfe looked everywhere to be sure that all the cigarettes were out; between thumb and forefinger he crushed the stubs one by one. We then went out and he locked the door, but he stood by the door like a man listening to a voice within; and unlocking it he said he would go back and be sure that no cigarette had been left burning. This he did. I concluded that I was in the presence of a man with a fire-phobia. He came out and locked the door. We descended to the street and a second time he went back. I waited for him, thinking of both of us: my principal phobia had been of water, in which several times as a child I almost drowned.

Elizabeth Nowell tells me that in his last years he showed no fear of fire, that indeed his desk and some of his papers were cigarette-burned. It may be that my surmise was wrong. But if wrong, there was another symbolism present, the nature of which eludes me. I still think that his strange behavior was in some way related to his father. In any case it reveals a great deal about the man, for he was wholly unaware that he was acting abnormally. His almost complete failure to understand the source and nature of the conflicts in him must be kept in mind, I think, by anyone who would understand him.

I never saw him in his last years. In 1939 Edward C. Aswell and his wife came through Idaho, and while we were drinking a cocktail she asked me what I thought would have happened to Wolfe, if he had lived. I said I thought he would have gone insane. I thought so because to the day of his death, so far as I know, he was not able to understand and discipline those tyrannical emotions that made him a wanderer among men. His wanderlust is not explained by his "great vitality" or his "search for truth." Somewhere he has written, "I feel at times as if I have developed a powerful monster, which will some day destroy me." Muller thinks that before his death "he had indeed made his peace, with his world and with himself." Another friend thinks that he had become quite aware "of the forces inside him" and that this will be proved by his letters, to be published soon by Scribner's. I shall remain unconvinced unless the letters show that he had become aware of the nature of his deep and tormenting attachment to his mother, and why he was so brutal to both her and Aline Bernstein.*

I have said that Wolfe and I talked but that was not the way of it at all. He once wrote his mother that "all of us talk too much." Wolfe talked incessantly and I listened. I had learned that most authors like to talk about themselves, and listen only when they have to. Now and then Wolfe would ask a question but he seldom gave me a chance to answer it. Now and then he would invite me to speak but always he interrupted me. He had almost no capacity to listen. This was not arrogance on his part. It was fear that he himself had no meaning to communicate, or would never be able to make the meaning plain.

I recall with not altogether pleasant emotions an evening I spent with him after he had returned from abroad. He told me about his experiences with Sinclair Lewis in England; and I think he had been phrasing the matter over and over in his mind, in the way of writers, because the story as he told it then was much like the version of it which later appeared in one of his novels. That evening, even more than in the published account — for time, I suppose, did something to soften the matter — his contempt for Lewis's histrionics was mad and wicked, though mixed with admiration.

The thing that had stirred him most deeply, I thought, was his realization that here was a novelist who had just won the highest honor in his field, yet seemed more bedeviled and unhappy than ever —a wanderer in Europe in search of he hardly knew what, and in any case of what he could never hope to find. Wolfe was haunted by the thought that the same fate would overtake him if he achieved such wealth and eminence; and he was thrown back again and again to *Ecclesiastes*. "Vanity!" he cried, his lips frothing and slobbering as they always did when he was deeply stirred. "Vanity, it is all vanity!" he howled, with utter contempt for the folly of human striving. But the child in him hoped nevertheless to find the Jeffers tower beyond tragedy, which Lewis had not found; some nobility in human nature that could stand serene and incorruptible above the accursed follies and vanities of egoism; some solace or sanctuary somewhere. His

---

*Having now read the letters I am still unconvinced.

31

emotions cried for it; his sharp cynical mind knew that it could not be, at least not in his lifetime, at least not for him.

I speak of his sharp cynical mind. He had that kind of mind but it looked out of a lonely adolescent innocence. He had a mind that probed deep into the motives of others and cast a pitiless light over his fellows; but I never felt that he was able to throw that light on himself. If he ever stood revealed to himself in its illumination his books nowhere show it. Muller speaks again and again of his passionate honesty and sincerity. No man can be honest and sincere without a pretty clear understanding of his own motives and nature. Wolfe the man was the protective and fierce guardian of Wolfe the child that filled the frame of Wolfe the man. The enormity of his blindness to himself, of his self-idolatry, is to be seen in all his novels, but in none more painfully than in the first. The most shocking and incredible instance of it, for me, is to be found in the fourth chapter.

The infant Eugene Gant lies in his crib, washed, powdered and fed, and thinking "quietly of many things before he dropped off to sleep." What does the infant Wolfe think about? About the "interminable sleep that obliterated time for him, and that gave him a sense of having missed forever a day of sparkling life." This babe was "heartsick with weary horror as he thought of the discomfort, weakness, dumbness, the infinite misunderstandings he would have to endure before he gained even physical freedom." He grew sick at heart thinking of the long life before him, the "lack of co-ordination of the centers of control, the undisciplined and rowdy bladder. . ." He suffered agonies because he could not talk. He looked at the sniggering relatives around him and "wondered savagely how they would feel if they knew what he really thought"; he had to "laugh at their whole preposterous comedy of errors"; and as they spoke to him words which he did not understand, the diapered baby saw that they were mangling them "in the preposterous hope" of making him understand; and "he had to laugh at the fools, in spite of his vexation." After the relatives went away leaving him in a shuttered room, this infant "saw his life down the solemn vista of a forest aisle, and he knew that he would always be the sad one." He knew that "he must always walk down lonely passages." He "understood that men were forever strangers to one another"; that they are "imprisoned in the dark womb. . . ."

He saw himself as "an inarticulate stranger, an amusing little clown. . . ." His "brain went black with terror."

In one of his essays Albert Jay Nock speaks of the "persistent human preference for pretense and make-believe over fact and truth, the persistent dislike and avoidance of realism." Wolfe was not of course a realist. The passage about the babe is the most fantastically unrealistic thing known to me in all of serious literature—so incredible in its failure to grasp the simplest realities, so maudlin in its glorifiication of the Wolfe-babe, that one doesn't know whether to be more astounded at Wolfe, who wrote it, or at book-reviewers, who accepted it (not a single one questioned it), or at Maxwell Perkins, who didn't throw it out. Perkins has written that Wolfe had "plenty of humor when the humor gland is functioning"; but the humor gland never functioned when he wrote about himself. As Muller points out, Eugene-Thomas is forever beside himself: he yells, howls, bellows madly, snarls like a wild beast, chokes with fury, turns white with constricted rage or frantic with horror. If he broods it is to contemplate things intolerable, implacable, unutterable. His favorite adjectives are wild, tortured, demented, demonic, maniacal. As Muller says, "extensive quotation is needless and depressing."

Such scenes as that of the babe offer one clue to Wolfe's personality. He simply gave to the infant the knowledge and perspective, the ironic and malicious reflections, of the twenty-seven-year old man. No other author known to me has so exalted and glorified himself while at the same time using the full power of his faculties to expose other people for what they are. He overcompensated because subconsciously he felt vile and worthless. He made himself his own god. But, as an American psychologist has said, talent should not be "used up in defensive distortions of self-healing in a constant kind of self-loving 'artistic hypochondriasis.' " He calls attention to the desire too common in artists to exhibit themselves rather than their art. That is the almost-fatal defect of many writers. As another psychologist puts it, some artists "spend much of their psychic energy maintaining and enhancing their fiction of superiority." If a protest reaction does not set in, "the individual's psychic energy will gradually become wholly directed toward the goal of superiority, he will lose self-perspective and arrive at a manifest egomania." Writing of John Huston, James

Agee says: "Huston lacks that deepest kind of creative impulse and that intense self-critical skepticism without which the stature of a great artist is rarely achieved." Intense self-critical skepticism Wolfe did not have.

Picasso has said that an artist paints "to unload himself of feelings and visions." Wolfe once said that an author writes a book to forget it. But he was never able to forget it. He was never able to write out of himself the tyrannies and clamorings, and proceed to more objective work. He belonged with those persons, among whom Samuel Johnson and Coleridge have been notable instances, whose personality is bigger than their art. Whether, if he had lived, his personality would eventually have yielded in service to his art we can never know. But I agree with Muller that emotional maturity would have been the death of him. He was essentially a poet. He had to throw off a million words of slag, to find the few that were always unalloyed gold.

* * *

Wolfe obsessed Wolfe. Self-pity was the disease in him. There is self-pity in any artist but in Wolfe it was a tyrant. *That* was the demon, if Mr. Muller must have one. His self-pity amazed me again and again, because when Wolfe looked into another man he looked into his soul. He looked into Sinclair Lewis deeper, I suspect, than Lewis ever looked into himself. Nobody who has read the brilliantly cruel chapters can doubt that he looked to the bottom of Maxwell Perkins. I felt time and again that he was looking to the bottom of me. It is, then, no less than astonishing that he was able to turn on himself only a reverent gaze that looked through mist and tears.

When reviews of his first book appeared and letters came from hometown folk his self-pity burst forth in scenes almost too painful to recall. Two or three times he came to me with a batch of letters and reviews, and he read them aloud, weeping, cursing, hating— hating as I have never seen a man hate. Sobbing, he would try to get out of him, to curse out, to vomit out, his heartbreak. If it was a critic who had leavened the good black bread of praise with some yeasty advice, Wolfe would gurgle and spit out his contempt: "The dull blighted unbuttoned blank-blank!" If it was a letter from his mother, rebuking, exhorting, pleading, scolding, he would shake his head sadly and stare down through his tears, saying, "She doesn't

34

understand!" If it was a letter of abuse and threats, his violent denunciations were unprintable.

I had published a novel at that time and a few of the reviews had stung. I was full of self-pity, too. An author who says that he is indifferent to reviews of his books is a philosopher, a fool, or a liar. Stupid or malicious reviews do hurt, even when the author knows that he should have only contempt for them. But I would have thought myself an awful ass to weep over them or to allow them to waste my energy. Muller gives that famous passage in which "a huge, naked, intolerable shame and horror pressed on Eugene . . . crushing and palpable like wet gray skies of autumn . . . hideous gray stuff filled him from brain to bowels . . . a naked stare from walls and houses . . . tasted it on his lips, endured it in the screaming and sickening dissonance of ten thousand writhing nerves . . . exhaustion . . . wild unrest. . . . He saw the whole earth with sick eyes, sick heart, sick flesh . . . writhing nerves of gray accursed weight of shame and horror . . . he could not die but must live hideously . . . forever in a state of retching and abominable nausea of heart, brain, bowels, flesh and spirit . . ."

Why? Because Eugene had just received his first rejection slip!

I felt deeply sorry for Wolfe, for I knew how he suffered; but I was amazed by the way he exploded, wept, and cursed. There he sat, his cheeks bathed, his eyes evil with contempt and hate and hurt, his loose wet lips pouring upon the "rats and vermin" all the vials of his wrath. "They all hate me," he said, "but I must go on! Vardis, we must go on! Don't ever let the low stinking bastards stop you!" He used a telling expression that he was to use again and again: "They're so damned little that they smell little." His hurt was absurd: on all his books he got a good press, even, with few exceptions, an effusive press.

What a man! What a lost and suffering child! When I was a boy my mother, too busy to be a mother herself, forced me to be parents, guardian, protector, and spiritual adviser to my brother who, having at the time a physical defect, was the victim everywhere of the bully boys. The urge to protect the weak, the crippled, the helpless was hugely overdeveloped in me. I wanted to go out and thresh Wolfe's "enemies" one by one. I see again his hands folding, crushing, destroying the offensive review or letter; his great shoulders hunched forward; his loose wet mouth, the mouth of the child, the orphan— lost, O lost!— to his people, to life, lost above all to himself; lost to the perspective and discipline which any artist must have; lost to that vigilant oversight without which the artist is the victim of his own spiritual corrosions and tyrannies. I still see those dark hurt eyes, wet and wicked, flickering with malice and spite; I can still feel his hot lusting for vengeance. He never forgot what he took to be a slight or a meanness and he never forgave it.

To his mother he wrote: "It takes me twenty-seven years to rise above the bitterness and hatred of my childhood." He had not risen above it. He hated with a depth and fixedness of purpose that I have never known in anyone else. One of his friends says, "You are dead right about the young Wolfe hating everything, but he didn't do this so much later when he was surer of himself." In the years when I knew him his hate was never focused and directed, never selective, with the result that it wore him out. He simply hated around him in all directions, and there were times—I knew this well—when he hated me. He adopted me, as he was to adopt Perkins, as a kind of mother —*not father, but mother.* His strongly feminine nature made that inevitable. I knew the two or three times he sought me out that he felt a need of me, of what seemed to him to be, but was not, my cool and well-disciplined inner core. I suppose I seemed to him to be quite austere, poised, at ease. Possibly for him I appeared to be one who had found the Jeffers tower beyond tragedy. But I had sense enough to realize that if I were with him too much our friendship would not endure. His affective tolerance was low.

His overdeveloped submissive tendencies had created in him a much greater need to give than to receive. Because of this, he was arrogantly demanding. Because of this, he was afraid of those toward whom he felt a strong urge to yield. He felt—subconsciously, of course, for if it had been conscious it would not have been such a problem—that if he went very far in giving, or *too far,* he would lose his individuality, of which, like me, he had none to spare. That subconscious fear is likely to be present in anyone, man or woman, whose overidentification with the opposite sex is tied up with overdevelopment of submissive tendencies. I speak as one of them, though

36

this in me I had not realized when I knew Wolfe. That in Wolfe explains why he could not be, why he dared not be, the lover of any woman very long. That, to anticipate, is the chief reason he left Perkins, whose nature also was strongly feminine. I have known only a few of Wolfe's friends but I should guess that the women in their attitudes and interests were quite masculine, that the men, like Perkins and me, were quite feminine, not in appearance in any case, but in intuitions and tastes. Those labor in vain who would understand the artist without recognizing this fundamental truth. All the nonsense written about Hemingway is an instance of what I mean.

Wolfe's feminine nature was so strong—with *his* childhood how could it have been otherwise?—that he was subconsciously tortured by threat of capitulation. It is this that at times made his egoism so offensive: *that* was only a defense against absorption of self by life, or, more narrowly, by people, such as mistresses with masculine strivings (which means only masculine identifications), toward whom such men, when unaware of their nature, are inevitably drawn, as Hemingway has been repeatedly, and I in my second marriage, and towards editors with contempt for women, whose own essentially feminine outlook aggravated Wolfe's deep anxieties, and heaped futility upon his efforts to find his maleness.

I early perceived some of these things in Wolfe. Or possibly I should say that I sensed them—sensed that his overpowering egoism was chiefly a defense against oversubmissiveness; that his fear of women grew out of the fact that he was too much woman himself; that his terrors and self-pity and overdramatizations were nourished by an unintegrated personality. I sensed them because these things were also in me and I was trying to understand them. I was careful to let him feel that I would put no demands on his precarious and almost tentative sense of self-adequacy. Wolfe could be held, if held at all, as friend or lover only by letting him back away when he felt stifled by his deep and abiding yearning to lay his heart at somebody's feet and his soul with it.

One of the psychologists alluded to above, Daniel E. Schneider, in *The Psychoanalyst and the Artist*, thinks that Wolfe was possibly the greatest American writer of his time but that "lyrical overplay" destroyed form in his work; and that without "monumental editorial help" it is doubtful that his work would have appeared in the form in which it appeared. From a phychologist writing about the artist, these statements it seems to me are a bit incredible. Wolfe's work does not have much form; his editors selected and rearranged the materials within the loose frame of the autobiographical chronicle. The lyrical overplay was the essence of Wolfe, and far from destroying form gave to his tales a kind of lyrical continuity. All his work lies in the pattern of the lineal flow of time and the river.

How important he was as a writer I do not pretend to know: this is not for any of us but for posterity to say. No one with tolerance of the brasses and cymbals in the music of emotions can fail to enjoy many of his scenes. I don't like, not even in my own work when these appear, exaggerations, emotional excesses, and character delineation in black and white. Auden says he had a "false conception of human nature," but Muller reminds us that after experimenting with various modern faiths, Auden "has returned to the doctrine of Original Sin!" Muller points out (what needs no pointing out to thinking people) that the notion of original sin is "as false to the actual complexities and paradoxes" of life as the opposite view of natural goodness. But it is true that in Wolfe's books people are awfully good, like Eugene, or awfully bad, like most of the others. Such a view is false.

*   *   *

Clifton Fadiman has said that Wolfe had the greatest command of language of any author of his time. On the contrary, language was in command of him. To one thing and to one alone did he give himself fully—not to food or drink or women or friendship, but to words. He suffered from overpraise. Canby says, for instance, that no scene, *no scene*, in *You Can't Go Home Again* could have been equalled by any other living writer! It is true that Wolfe had enormous talent for creating profane, vulgar, rowdy, boisterous scenes in which most of the characters are heels. But he overdid it. His talent in character was that of caricature. His talent in scene was "romantic." His talent in language was too largely an undiscriminating engulfing of Roget.

Muller thinks he came close to the creation of the American myth.* He certainly belonged to his country. Like it, he grossly and

---

*It seems to me that myth is produced not by one person but by the folksoul: see "The Novelist and his Background," ahead.

lustily exaggerated everything, including his love-making, hungers, strivings, torments, ambitions, and plans. His cultists were busy before he died converting him to a prodigious legend. In a book that I have published on writing, I put it this way:

"He was, of course, the kind of man who is born and built for the myth-makers. Too huge for ordinary beds or clothes or automobiles, too tall for ordinary windows and doors, he came on the American scene with a book to match his size; and Americans, with their interest in bigness of all kinds, took him to their hearts. With the publication of his first book the myth started, and he pitched in to help it grow. One of the themes running through his volumes is to be found in the word devour. At once the Wolfe protagonist began to devour everything in sight—books, food, women, drink, far places, and indeed everything that a titan could feed on. All things from then on were oversized, and from wonder to wonder the size grew. Little men gazed at him with rapt astonishment. Little women placed themselves in the way of easy capture. And he took everything as his right. He was becoming a legend, and to fertilize the legend he made his manuscripts bigger and bigger; and the mythmakers got busy with these also, spreading the story that they were delivered by truck in enormous bales. Wolfe tried to become a symbol of what he thought was his country's meaning. I sat with him one morning at breakfast when he devoured enough for ten men. He wolfed it down, to use another of his favorite words; but observing him I was not at all persuaded that he was conscious of eating. He was simply taken over body and soul by the job of being big.

"That is all right but for the fact that Wolfe was being defeated by the legend. If he had lived it would have been fascinating to watch the labors of the legend-makers, as the legend developed. It was engulfing him, and in trying to fill the stupendous vacuum he was losing sight of the man. He was in danger of losing sight of life itself and going off into the stratosphere like a wandering nebula. Because the mythmakers destroy what they build, as in all times past they destroyed their gods. The thing created is at last swallowed by its over-zealous creators. In ancient times people ate their gods, and, later, their god-surrogates, such as the bull and lamb; and today they create

39

the myth-god only to devour it. It takes an artist of tough fiber to develop in his votaries a case of indigestion. . . ."

I sent those words to Elizabeth Nowell and she rapped my knuckles. She says Wolfe did nothing to fertilize the legend. But what does Perkins say? "He seems to feel a certain shame at the idea of turning out a book of reasonable dimensions." Edward C. Aswell, who became his second editor, has confessed that he made three books out of a pile of manuscript "eight feet high." If we allow two inches to the ream there must have been 20,000 pages.

He was trying to create something big, and very possibly he had the talent for it, if that talent could have been disciplined and directed; but as things turned out he is for me one of the American tragedies of our time. He is a tragedy in a country whose romantic excesses suffocate its sense of the realities; whose love of freedom is less than its love of power; whose devotion to duty is less than its devotion to self-righteousness; and whose whole notion of truth is Paul's rather than the Preacher's. Among so much that is superficial and shoddy, Wolfe was never able to find his bearings; and, rebelling against the cynical wisdom and weariness of such men as Perkins, he fled into the adolescent cloudland of apostrophe. Those who would know some of the best and a good deal of the worst in what Muller calls the American myth can go to his books, for better than any other writer he set it down. In the last chapters of *You Can't Go Home Again* they can find a callow sentimentalism that is appalling, until they come to the last six lines, when they will see this land and this writer at their magnificent best.

I never saw Wolfe after 1930 or 1931 (I cannot now be sure of the year). He was then going abroad. He put out a big hand to clasp mine and said, "Vardis, don't let the sons of bitches lick you. Keep fighting. . ." When he turned away his eyes were wet.

In the year of his death he stopped off in Boise and tried to find me but failed. He spread legends as he journeyed. He must have said, for instance (for the story has come to me from Santa Fe, Salt Lake City, and Portland), that when we were teaching colleagues we got as drunk as owls, to screw up the courage to face our classes. We were never drunk together, but it is true that we both detested teaching. Once or twice I happened to see him hesitating at the classroom door, or he happened to see me, and to one another we confessed our folly with a selfconscious grin.

It was in such moments that my heart went out to him, for then the child stood forth, naked and defenseless. It is in such moments that I like to remember him.

Thomas Wolfe and Maxwell Perkins

In an essay in *The Writer's Book,* produced by the Authors Guild, Mr. Thomas R. Coward of Coward-McCann wrote: "Perkins' understanding of and hold on his authors was such that, as the literary world knows, Thomas Wolfe left him, crying that he was bewitched." I sent Mr. Coward's statement to one who knew Wolfe well and got this reply: "Wolfe left Perkins because he was *un*bewitched." Herbert J. Muller, in his book on Wolfe, points out that Wolfe thought George Webber no longer lost, no longer in need of a foster father, "but this does not explain why he must part with his editor and friend." One reason, Mr. Muller thinks, was "simple embarrassment: Wolfe had reached the stage in his narrative where he had to deal with his relations with Perkins and Scribner's." Muller finds another reason in De Voto's stinging remark that Wolfe could not write a novel without help. The one who corrected Mr. Coward above writes me that Wolfe "always had to have somebody to be his receptacle for all his woes and blunders and mistakes—and I think maybe one reason for his leaving Perkins was that the receptacle had got filled up." That, I think, comes closer to the heart of the matter. But the real reason,

---

*First published in *Tomorrow,* July, 1951.

of which all the other reasons commonly given seem to me to be only symptoms, lay much deeper, and so far as I know has never been suggested by anyone. I am aware that the forthcoming Wolfe letters may modify my view** of the Wolfe-Perkins relationship, may indeed show that the receptacle got so filled up that Wolfe had to turn elsewhere; but I doubt that all the eloquent self-pity which I expect to find in the letters will appreciably alter the conclusions set forth here.

It is well first to try to understand the nature of the two men. I saw Perkins only briefly a time or two and my impression of him was not favorable. At Wolfe's urging I offered to Scribner's the manuscript of *In Tragic Life* and saw Perkins a few days later when he rejected and returned the script to me. Wolfe told me that neither Perkins nor anyone else in the House read it. I thought Perkins a suspicious, unhappy, aloof, and quite austere person, and I wondered why between him and Wolfe there was such a strong attachment.

By nature Maxwell Perkins was essentially feminine. His photographs suggest it. His letters prove it. John Hall Wheelock***, in his excellent introduction to the letters in *Editor to Author*, says Perkins had a delicacy of feeling *almost* feminine. In him the Puritan and Cavalier, shrewd Yankee and "generous and disarming artist were subtly and perpetually at war." He was "shy but very daring"; he had a Vermonter's distaste "for the display of emotion in music and poetry"; and "male dancers embarrassed him." He had "mistrust of human nature at its present level and of all callow idealism"—such as Wolfe's, for instance; and he had a tough New England conscience.

The letters reveal these things and many more. They reveal his adolescent interest in war and military strategy, which with childlike innocence he loved to share with such as Hemingway. They reveal his contempt for women. He wrote Edward Bok: "You have practically confessed . . . to a rather low opinion of women (an opinion to which I have no objection, since I share it) . . .." No intelligent, sensitive, educated man has a low opinion of women who is not in

---

** They did not.
*** Acknowledgment is made of Mr. Wheelock's permission to use materials from his Introduction and the letters.

unconscious revolt against the feminine coloring in his nature. Perkins wrote James Boyd: "I am still always scared when confronted by a charming young woman." He wrote William B. Wisdom: "I think you know that we have five girls. It just seemed incredible to me that I should have any girls at all, and I always thought there would be a boy." If it was incredible to him that he should have had any girls *at all,* with what consternation he must have watched their coming, one after another! There is our clue. Of his attitude toward his wife and five daughters certain chapters in *You Can't Go Home Again* give a brilliant and not very sympathetic picture.

His contempt for women (which means for himself) and his youthful interest in all the trappings of warfare (which means his sense of inadequacy as a male) are enough to suggest the nature of Perkins. On what Wolfe was like I have already written and shall here mention only those traits which are important to an understanding of the relationship. In a penetrating essay on the psychology of the artist Dr. Beatrice Hinkle reminds us of this quite obvious truth: "In the psychology of the artist we have the masculine counterpart of woman's creativeness." She means, of course, that all male artists are essentially feminine—not, as a friend persists in writing me, effeminate, no, but feminine—and need "an adequate subjective relation" with a woman for the quickening of their creative product.

* * *

Wolfe was also essentially feminine in his nature. With the kind of childhood he had, how could he have been otherwise?—for he was his mother's youngest, her pet and darling, her baby, and his attachment to her was of course the most tormenting but also the deepest and most abiding in his life. That attachment, and his failure to understand, or apparently even to suspect it, made him the kind of man he was, and developed in him his self-defensive traits, none of which was stronger than his self-pity.

"Tom," Perkins wrote him, "you ought not to say some of the things you do—that I find your sufferings amusing and don't take them seriously. . . . Do try to turn your mind from them and try to arouse your humor, because to spend dreadful hours brooding over them, and in denunciation and abuse on account of them, seems to be only to aggravate them. It does no good." But such sound advice was lost on Wolfe. When he was sued for libel, Perkins tells us that "he simply could not take it. It was for that reason that we settled the lawsuit, although we never did tell him so." Wolfe was so tormented that he could only "drink and brood"—and blame anybody in the world but himself. Having almost no capacity to perceive and admit in himself weakness or error, or to believe that even his wildest impulses were anything but purest truth, he blamed Perkins and Scribner's.

His self-pity was the source of his belief that he was persecuted, that he had enemies everywhere, that he was misunderstood and underrated, yes, and underpaid. His preoccupation with money became so obsessive that one who has written about him says he one day broke down in tears crying that he had never had a bank account. That obsession led to some of his most unworthy acts. In 1936, for instance, he was angrily writing Perkins that he had been overcharged for author's corrections in *The Story of a Novel*. Apparently he did a lot of revising in proof; he exceeded his allowance by $1,100, and we must bear in mind that Scribner's were remarkably generous in this, giving an author 20% for corrections instead of the customary 10%. Revealing is this sentence in the Perkins reply: "If I gave you the impression that I thought this was unfair [i.e., for Wolfe to pay the $1,100], it came from my dread of the resentment I knew you would feel to have them deducted from your royalties." Perkins tried to explain the matter to him—how many times he had tried to explain it before!—and concluded: "I have never doubted your sincerity and never will. I wish you could have felt that way toward us."

I would not imagine that the letters now published tell more than a small part of all the hours Perkins spent trying to convince Wolfe that he was not being robbed. That Wolfe had the notion that as an artist he was entitled to large sums of money is revealed again and again in his letters to his mother. He took her earnings for his own use, with no shame at all, and carried this attitude over to Scribner's. The reason he did so may become clear as we proceed.

Wolfe had F. D. Roosevelt's sense of destiny—that is, his prodigious vanity, and interest in what the future would say about him; and with the most appalling indifference to the feelings of others he left records of certain relationships with women, for the amazement and delight of posterity. These have been destroyed. Though the Perkins letters give no hint of it, we may suspect that Perkins found Wolfe's adolescent attitude toward women rather offensive. He was too wise and worldly, of course, not to have known that most artists do not feel themselves governed by certain social laws, which are assumed to apply to all people.

Possibly we may summarize the two men in such terms as these: Wolfe's sensitivity drove him to excesses, Perkins' to fastidious seclusion; Wolfe's to preposterous exaggerations, Perkins' to subtle understatement; Wolfe's to gargantuan bad taste, Perkins' to a delicately nourished sense of the rights of others; Wolfe's to size and Perkins' to quality. In a way they compensated and balanced one another. For a while they must have been absorbed by fascinated study of one another, the one so egocentric and selfishly headlong, the other almost chillingly sophisticated and self-controlled; the one (one judges from his letters) a perfect gentleman, the other (in some moods, at least) an insufferable boor.

An important but minor difference between them, and one that aroused both to increasing impatience with one another, was their irreconcilable political views. Perkins was a Republican. Wolfe was a wild-eyed and shaggy-headed radical. Though one of Wolfe's friends would play this down and find it of little significance, the Perkins letters clearly reveal that political differences played a part in the final break. Wolfe's triumphant but painfully callow conclusion in *You Can't Go Home Again* leaves no room for doubt.

When Wolfe was sued for libel he told Perkins "at great length, and with overwhelming eloquence, of the injustice done him on all hands in this blank blank country — Germany was white as snow in contrast with it — where the honest men are all robbed and bludgeoned by scoundrels. And it all wound up with, 'And now you have got me into a $135,000 libel suit!' " Such a self-pitying and unrealistic sense of injustice has characterized a number of American intellectuals, who have gone with Communism in one way or another. Wolfe wanted to go and came close to going.

"In a way," Perkins wrote Marjorie Kinnan Rawlings in 1940, "that was one of the issues between Tom and me, and I kept telling him that what he felt would come through his writing, even though not specifically stated. And yet he wanted at that time to be a Communist, the last thing that he truly was . . ." What period is meant by "at that time" is not clear, but as early as 1930 Wolfe was playing with the thought of joining the Communists. He was then trying to determine where he stood politically, and to understand the function of the artist in a world filled with darkness at noon. Two or three times he talked to me about it; I thought his interest very superficial but it seems to have grown after I last saw him and to have become a source of anxiety to Perkins. Early in 1937 Perkins wrote him: "I did try to keep you from injecting radical, or Marxian, beliefs in 'Time and the River,' because they were your beliefs in 1934 and 1935, and not those of Eugene Gant in the time of the book." It appears that Wolfe had been reproaching him for having cut, and, as Wolfe saw it, for having almost destroyed *Of Time and the River*; and in this long letter Perkins defends himself: "I know your memory is a miracle, but it seems as if you must have forgotten how we worked and argued." Some of the arguments were unquestionably about political matters. According to Mr. Wheelock, a Perkins correspondent "asserted that Wolfe had turned against Perkins on the ground that the latter was a believer in the capitalist system." Wheelock thinks this correspondent got the idea from the long letter to Perkins which concludes *You Can't Go Home Again*.

* * *

He had found (Wolfe writes in this conclusion and farewell) that down below were the forgotten "Helots, who with their toil and blood and suffering unutterable" supported the wealthy men who took their luxuries for granted. Then came the crash, and Wolfe caught the "vision of man's inhumanity to man" when "the disinherited of America" found their food in garbage cans, their warmth in foul latrines, their sleep in subway corridors. He had learned that Perkins was the Preacher, the Pessimist; he now realized that "I believe in everything you say, but I do not agree with you." What was the mystery of "our eventual cleavage and our final severance?" The "little tongues will wag . . . they will propose a thousand quick and ready explanations . . . but really, Fox, the root of the whole thing is here."

Is where? "To lose the earth you know, for greater knowing; to lose the life you have, for greater life; to leave the friends you loved, for greater loving; to find a land more kind than home, more large than earth — Whereon the pillars of this earth are founded, toward which the conscience of the world is tending — a wind is rising, and the rivers flow." How beautifully he put it, but did he understand what he was writing? He looks back to a letter in which Perkins had written, "I know you are going now. I always knew that it would happen. I will not try to stop you, for it had to be. And yet, the strange thing is, the hard thing is, I have never known another man with whom I was so profoundly in agreement in all essential things." We may suspect that the "father" was there speaking out of hurt, and hardly knew what he was saying; for what he says there was simply not true. Yes, says Wolfe, that *is* the strange, hard, wonderful, mysterious thing; but even though they agreed, Perkins was the North Pole, he the South, and between them lay the whole world. If they agreed on all essential things, "why, then, the struggle that ensued, the severance that has now occurred?" Why is Wolfe now making "my farewell to you . . . the parent and guardian of my spirit in its youth, the thing has happened and we know it. Why?"

Does Wolfe have the answer? "I know the answer, and the thing I have to tell you now is this—" Is what? That he refuses to "be confirmed to more fatality." He had to leave Perkins, he tells us, because of all the men he had known Perkins was the most "fatally resigned." He tells us that Perkins accepted things as they were, and in the next moment speaks of the mighty Perkins effort to change them! In short, Wolfe put his finger on nothing and made nothing clear. He can tell us only that they had to part because Perkins believed that man is fashioned for a day; Wolfe, that he is fashioned for eternity.

Perkins was Ecclesiastes, the Fatalist and Pessimist, cynical, wise, tolerant, resigned; Wolfe was eternal Youth and Hope, the Optimist, who said that evils need not be and must not be. Perkins was the Republican, the Capitalist, the evil Princeling at the top; and Wolfe, looking back to his "dark" days in Brooklyn, was the impassioned voice of the disinherited, of the horribly suffering helots; and out of his great sense of justice he cried to Perkins that there must be equality and a brotherhood of man.

The story is as old as human history, but is it the answer? That is the answer Wolfe gives, and some who have thrilled to his callow romanticism have thought it answer enough. Now the curious truth — and it is often this way — is that at heart Wolfe was more Republican, capitalist, and princeling than Perkins could ever have been. One need not have known Wolfe, one need only read his letters, to find the painful and abundant proof of his arrogance, contempt, love of luxuries, and a view of himself as a privileged person. This long self-righteous letter to Perkins reveals not Perkins but Wolfe, and it reveals Wolfe *in revolt against those things in himself, unperceived by him, which he pretends to find and condemn in his friend.* In psychological jargon this is called projection.

Another reason given for the severance (and it was a reason, though a minor one) was Wolfe's wish to put Perkins and some of the other people at Scribner's in his novels. Now it is true that the sensitive Perkins did not want to be written about. The proof of this is conclusive.

Wolfe at one time intended to do a profile of Perkins for *The New Yorker.* Perkins was horrified. Wolfe was prevailed on to abandon the project. Later, Malcolm Cowley did a Perkins profile, which appeared in April, 1944; and in a letter to one whose name Mr. Wheelock suppresses, Perkins wrote: "I can tell you that profiles in *The New Yorker* are things to dread. I dreaded this one for a couple of years, and even consulted a lawyer as to what means might be taken to prevent its publication. But when it did come out, I said, 'I wouldn't mind being like that fellow,' and secretly thought he was a great sight better person than myself."

These philosophical musings lead Perkins to one of the finest passages in his letters. The harm done in the world, he believed, is not the work of deliberately evil people, but of those who are so sure that they are good and that God is with them that nothing can stop them. He thought Hitler was such a person, Luther another, and Henry Wallace a third; that Wallace would be "perfectly ready to take charge of the whole universe, with the certainty that

he could manage it . . . The world is crowded with Good people."
Among the Good people Wolfe counted himself one.

As late as 1937 Perkins wrote Wolfe that he still did not understand why Wolfe had left him, "but that need make no difference
between us, and I won't let it on my side. Miss Nowell should never
have told you of my concern as to your writing about *us* . . ."
Elizabeth Nowell was Wolfe's agent. It is clear that she told Perkins that Wolfe wanted to write about the Scribner people, and
that Perkins expressed concern. It is also clear that after the break,
Wolfe behaved like a sulking child. Perkins wrote Hamilton Basso,
"It is ridiculous of him to refuse to come face to face and forget
all about the trouble."

We do not know just how important this matter was. Perkins,
a Vermont Yankee, must have been terribly distressed on learning
that Wolfe was going to write about him and his colleagues. Yet
he should have anticipated it, and possibly did. Wolfe had to write
about his friends, and he had to write about them, for the most part,
in terms that were not flattering. We can imagine, then, the distress
which Perkins felt, and the discussions which he had with Miss Nowell, another New Englander who, I think, accepted his view.* Perkins
seems to have been prepared to accept anything that might be written about him, but not about his associates. He wrote Wolfe: "I
know the difficulty of your problem and I never meant this point
to come up to confuse you. But don't you see that serious injury
to this House and to my long-time associates here, for which I was
responsible, would make me wish to be elsewhere? I hate to speak
about this, but I can't have you misunderstand it."

In no point of their relationship is Perkins more vulnerable than
here. He was absurd if he imagined that Wolfe could do serious
injury to Scribner's, and he was guilty of moral cowardice if he accepted without protest Wolfe's writing about many living persons,
some of them known to Perkins, and balked the moment Wolfe pro-
posed to invade the inner Perkins circle. If Wolfe was forced to a
choice between leaving Scribner's or not writing about Scribner

---

*Miss Nowell's letters to me reveal that she thought that in these two essays
I had written too frankly about Wolfe and the Wolfe-Perkins relationship.

people, those on the side of both truth and art must find him justified in leaving.

* * *

Another reason given for the break is tactfully understated by Mr. Wheelock: "Perhaps Wolfe felt that the current rumor that he was unable to get his books into final form without the help of Perkins, reflected upon him as a writer. In any case, he was unhappy about the situation, and was inclined to blame Perkins for the extraordinary help Perkins had given him in the organizing and shaping of his material." To say that Wolfe was unhappy and inclined to blame Perkins, and that he felt the situation reflected upon him, is to put it in the gentlest terms possible. Perkins says, "Tom *demanded* help. He *had* to have it. No one who did not know him could possibly understand it, but he would get into such a state of desperation." Perkins gave the help with "very great reluctance and anxiety." And matters seem not to have been improved after Wolfe left Perkins and went to Edward C. Aswell. Wolfe still thought his books finished when they were, Perkins says, "not at all" and "he expected to work with Aswell as he had with me." Aswell, Perkins tells us, had the same anxiety, and no doubt had his patience pushed to the extremest limits.

As Perkins reveals the matter to us, he and Wolfe argued endlessly over what should or should not be cut out of his huge piles of script. I knew Wolfe well enough to understand that anything taken out of his story he would have thought a mutilation of his spirit and a theft of his meaning. It is impossible to believe that he could ever have forgiven the cutting. Indeed, he came more and more to feel bitterness and resentment because of the help he demanded and had to have; to feel that he was controlled and not his own master; and to approach the point of open revolt after the rumor spread that without great assistance he could never have done a novel at all.

Mr. Weelock tells us that when Perkins faced a delicate situation he wrote by hand. He did so to Wolfe in a short note in November, 1936, after learning that Wolfe intended to leave him. This note reveals deep perturbation. In fact he sent a second note the day after the first and in this he said, "I have never doubted for

51

your future on any grounds except, at times, on those of your being able to control the vast mass of material you have accumulated . . . You seem to think I have tried to control you. I only did that when you asked my help and then I did the best I could. It all seems very confusing to me."

In these notes one *feels* the deep hurt in Perkins. After dispatching the second note he seems almost at once to have written a third, also in longhand, in which he said, "for we do not know how we have done that; or where you refer to 'exerting control of a man's future,' which we have no intention of doing at all, and would not have the power or right to do." Three weeks later he revealed his hurt in a letter to Hemingway (a Perkins weakness was writing too frankly about authors to other authors); but not until January 13, at least in the letters published, did he return to the matter of "control." Then in a long letter he went so far as to say: "If you wished it, we would publish any book by you as written except for such problems as those which prohibit — some can't be avoided but I don't foresee them. Length could be dealt with by publishing in sections. Anyhow, apart from physical or legal limitations not within the possibility of change by us, we will publish anything as you write it."

We will publish anything as you write it. That is complete surrender: gone are the problems of 'serious injury' to his long-time associates, his own morbid dread of being written about, and his guiding conscience in the work of a man who by himself was not an artist. Did Perkins make these astonishing concessions because he did not want his publishing House to lose Wolfe, or because he himself did not want to lose him? Was his motive *business* or *love*? I do not know, but the latter would be my guess. Meanwhile, Wolfe seems to have written Perkins that Perkins ought to search himself; and January 14 Perkins replied: "But what a task you've put to me, to search myself — in whom I'm not so very much interested any more." This letter from Wolfe filled twenty-eight pages, and Perkins replied in one that runs to almost two thousand words.

"You were never overruled," he wrote Wolfe. "Do you think you are clay to be moulded? I never saw anyone less malleable." He had said to Wheelock (he tells Wolfe), "Maybe it's the way Tom is. Maybe we should just publish him as he comes and in the end it will be all right." We need not expect to find Perkins wholly honest in such statements; after all, he had a most difficult problem —he was dealing with a child, with whom he could not possibly have laid all the cards on the table. If they had published the books just as Wolfe wrote them, "and the results had been bad at the moment, would you not have blamed me? Certainly I should have bitterly blamed myself." Elsewhere, with *Of Time and the River* in mind, he wrote: "What I have done has destroyed *your* belief in it and you must not act inconsistently with the fact." After Wolfe's death, Perkins read a book about editors and publishers in which it was charged (as Wheelock puts it) that Wolfe " had been the helpless victim of his editors, who had cut and mangled his work." On the contrary, as Wheelock says, Perkins "had sacrificed time and health in an effort to help him." No one but a rabid Wolfe partisan could doubt it. Nobody can doubt that without an editor like Perkins Wolfe would never have been published at all. What a pathetic story it is of ingratitude in the author, and hurt in the editor who labored with such devotion to bring a talent to fruition! Why did the misunderstanding have to be?

The publication of my tetralogy brought many letters from men, most of them young, who confessed that they were Vridars. After the passing of many years there one day came to me the realization that for all my male friends but one or two I had been a father or mother. I mentioned this to my psychologist-brother, who said impatiently, "I sometimes wonder if you novelists are as simple as you seem to be." To an able psychologist who had been in practice a quarter of a century, it may be that most novels looked like something that Alice found under the "golden bough" in wonderland.

* * *

The reasons that have been given here for the break between Wolfe and Perkins cannot be dismissed, but they are the symptoms or results and not the source of the problem. The source was the obvious fact that Perkins became for Wolfe a mother-substitute, and Wolfe became for Perkins the son he had hoped for. If both men had understood the nature of their relationship, it might have endured, and have been a source of spiritual health for both of them.

Whether Perkins ever looked into the deeper emotions involved I cannot say. That Wolfe did not is certain. If he had understood the nature of their friendship before he left Perkins he would not have written the letters he wrote just after he left. If he had understood it years later when, facing death, he wrote the farewell note to Perkins, he would have written a different kind of note.

Wolfe's odyssey, his restless and almost continuous wandering, was a symbolic effort to free himself from his mother — to be able to return home again, not as the child but as the adult man. What do those who write all around Wolfe's problem think he meant by the words, "You can't go home again"? How desperately he strove to — and not to! What tantrums and furies and mad language his problem threw up from his subconscious mind! How it drove him year after year, until a train, a river, a pilgrimage, a wind became for him a symbol of escape and freedom! In the year of his death he had abandoned Europe, for the time being anyway, and was exploring his homeland in an effort, less frenzied than formerly, but still drawing from his subconscious depths, to find himself. One of his friends thinks he had found peace. Possibly he had found a plateau, a period of relative quiet, a temporary easing of his turmoil and fret. If he had lived he might have blown the dam and found himself. With what humility would he then have gone, pride and arrogance in hand, to make his peace with his editor and friend!

He fled continuously from his mother. He fled from his friends. He had to flee as long as he could not explore, determine, and face his problem. He had to leave Perkins. He had to leave him because, for Wolfe, who carried his heart in his throat and his childhood in his eyes, the relationship had become too intimate and suffocating. He used exactly the right word when he said he felt that he was being controlled. His mother had controlled him as a child, idolized him, fussed and fretted over him, with the result that he developed abnormal dependence on her. His problem was to *realize* himself as an adult standing free and alone in his own strength. Until he could understand that problem — indeed, that he *had* a problem — he had to rebel against every mothering person, lest, loathing himself, he abjectly surrender, and return, defeated, as a child to Asheville. How he must have winced when it was said that he could not write a novel without help! And since Perkins (this is revealed in his letters) hungered for a son, we may assume that in ways, most likely unperceived by him, he did try to control Wolfe, did try to give him form and direction, in the way of devoted parents everywhere.

No doubt Wolfe's relationship with Perkins was in the beginning casual enough. Wolfe's agent offered a manuscript to Scribner's, while Wolfe was abroad. Perkins read a part of it and put it aside, and might never have read all of it (I think Mr. Wheelock suggests this, or it may be Professor Cargill) if another member of the House had not got interested in it. Anyway it was accepted, Perkins knowing all the while that he would have to spend a lot of time to get it in publishable shape. The two men met, and began to work together over the story. The well-disciplined Perkins, intellectually cool, precise, and with a quick grasp of pattern and form, must have appealed enormously to Wolfe, who had great need of such virtues. The impulsive Wolfe, childlike, naive, eloquent, idealistic, visionary, must have appealed enormously to Perkins, whose own emotional fires were so well-tended and subdued that he was repelled by display of emotion in music and poetry. The relationship developed into one between artist and critic, Job and the Preacher, mother and child. The control which Perkins imposed, and which it was necessary to impose, Wolfe accepted and endured until fame and fortune came his way. Then he rebelled, and his rebellion was nourished by rumors of his helplessness, and the sneers of certain critics. One could wish that he had gone to a good psychiatrist. Instead, his self-protective illusions conspired to make him believe that Perkins was destroying him. Unaware of the nature of his problem, even unaware, it may be, that he had a problem, he had to believe that Perkins was destroying him, or surrender his self-respect, his soul and his will.

But what a pity that it all had to end that way!

The Advantages in Being Modest

I'm such a modest person that writing about myself in full view of the world, without the customary disguises, brings to my face the pallor of humility. It is said by some that there are books in my name in which I am the principal character, and if this is so it suggests that I am not as modest as I pretend to be. It has also been pointed out that I have said in print that modesty is a bogus virtue. I have sometimes thought it a vice, for the reason that a polite and carefully nourished self-effacement is not, as the prima donnas could tell us, the easiest way to become famous. Nor is it exactly the kind of thing that the human ego wants. Indeed, it possibly can be set down as a fact that the person who makes a profession of being modest, as some think I have done, does not find any of the stages available to him large enough on which to strut. Rather than exhibit himself in surroundings too mean for his talents, he prefers to hide in the wings and look out.

I don't know whether I am as modest as that. I do know that I became alarmed, many years ago, by the strenuous and unresting demands of my ego. Through a tortuous series of evasions I arrived at the conclusion that I would have to laugh at my pretensions or seek a psychiatrist. I chose the former and Mr. Oscar Levant the latter, and I suspect that the way of things with me has been no more severe than with him.

Modesty, a bearded authority has said, begins in fear — in the fear of being appraised at less than one's worth. All is not gold that glitters, nor is everything genius that hides its light under a bushel. The modest person, if he is cunning — and if he is not cunning he will be a failure at being modest — learns early in life that a charming self-effacement is the most sovereign of all defenses. It can, in fact, be devastating attack. If in a group you choose to be silent and to hide a full or vacant mind behind a Mona Lisa smile, you will find, before the evening is over, that accusing stares will be turned on you by those who did all the talking. They may have been, in Meredith's words, like a brook, shallow but always rippling; but they have learned a few things, too. They have learned, for instance, that silent persons are universally held in awe. They have heard the old adage that still waters run deep.

If they look accusingly at the silent one, it may be only because so many "schools" of psychology have bewildered and abashed all but the reckless. Or it may be that they can see no reason why silence should wear an enviable prestige all its own and are fed up with the notion that the one who sits back, aloof and bored, is wiser that those who chatter. It is strange, once you think of it, that so many people assume that the silent one is not empty, as in fact he often is, but keeps his mouth shut because the weighty matters dwelling in his cortex might not be understood. Once in a great while that may be so. But usually the silent one does not speak because prolonged admiration of self has left him nothing to say.

It does not follow that the chatterbox has anything to say, either. But he is not our problem at the moment. Our problem is the author of this essay who wishes to tell why during his long and humble life he has been one of the modest ones, and what he has got, or anyone with a talent for such caprice can hope to get, out of it. He can hope to get more than the awe of persons who suspect him of omniscence. If he has the cunning to manage the thing properly, he can protect himself against embarrassing mistakes. Nobody, I have observed, can talk a half-hour without revealing more ignorance than

57

knowledge; and it is what we don't know rather than what we know that our friends as well as our enemies choose to remember. There is so much frustration and envy in all of us that we are more interested, when lending an ear to others, in catching them in error than in learning from them. And if we find them ignorant, as most talkative persons are, there is also for us, in addition to the enhancement of our self-esteem, the luxury of pity.

That, I think, is about the nicest of all luxuries. Pity of others is, some of the psychologists would tell us, only a form of self-aggrandizement. And of course they're right. It is one of the commonest tricks with which we try to believe that we are human beings, and not merely a part of that subnormal mass out of which, Albert Jay Nock's friend told him, the occasional human being emerges. Those who seem to be superior we may envy, or fear and hate; those who seem to be inferior we can look down on, as privately as we wish, and accord the socially approved vice of pity.

The novelist who aims to be popular knows all that. He knows that a novel, if it is to be widely acclaimed, must do one of two things — either portray cardboard figures whom the reader will envy and whose lives he will vicariously usurp; or figures whom he can pity. Of the two I don't know which is more assured of popular success; I suspect that with competent craftsmanship either can make a man rich, if assiduously pursued. In the one we have unrealistic enhancement of human traits and yearnings that are generally admired; in the other we have poor white or colored trash, the okies and mice and men. One of the major fallacies of the present age is the notion that human beings love one another and that their fantastic tolerance of uncontrolled birth, even at subnormal levels, is an expression of that love, whereas in fact it is an expression of fear and anxiety. If you have lived in small communities where everybody knows everybody, you have learned that almost nobody loves anybody. The allergies develop on sight, let alone on touch.

Now the luxury of pity is one advantage which the modest person is quick to seize. If you will observe him in a group, aloof and silent and watchful, you will see pity in every sneering and condescending line of his face. You will, that is, if he has not learned to act well. The modest person who has not mastered his role often looks complacent, or contemptuous, or now and then repulsively arrogant. Such a one has no right to enter a role which, when played well, calls for a subtle and gracious self-effacement above the still waters running deep.

There are so many advantages which the modest person harvests — more than this short essay has time for, or its author has had the sagacity to discover. For my own part I was sternly taught as a child to be seen, occasionally, and never heard. I learned at an early age that nearly everybody wants to talk, and I think that before adolescence I must have been a pretty sharp observer and an intent listener. By the time I was grown I had seen and heard so much and learned so much that any desire I was born with to talk had been so thoroughly hushed that only alcohol thereafter would ever lift it out of hiding. I learned, for instance, that it is a rare person who is willing to listen if his ignorance and prejudices are to be ruffled. If persons do listen, politely enough, to the countless lecturers who traipse from lectern to lectern, to the commencement orators, to the thousands recruited from all possible places to talk at luncheons to the millions who belong to the clubs for bearded boys, it is not because they care a hoot about what is said; and you will invariably find that the matters that elicit their laughter, approval, or applause are happily of a pattern with their beliefs and prejudices. Americans have so little education in any reasonable sense of that word and such fantastic notions of what education is, along with a depressed feeling of being culturally undernourished, that they have got the habit of listening every year to as many speakers as their program chairmen can find. This custom, so peculiarly American, of sitting in bad air on hard chairs and being bored to death in the name of culture, is exactly like that of changing clothes with the styles, switching from one popular idol to another, and picking up habits from the incessant whine of the radio commercials.

The modest person who was told to shut up as a child has learned the hard way that nobody wants to hear him talk, even if they are paying for it. On every possible occasion the truth of this has been as plain as open mouths before me. Typical of such experiences was a writers' conference I attended; at the dinner table a group of children, ranging in age from thirty-five to sixty, and including such celebrities as Caroline Gordon, Stephen Spender, and Malcolm Cowley, competed for the attentive ears of this author and his wife and Mrs. Cowley, who had also learned that silence is golden. Listening to such rather lovable, self-indulgent, clamorous children, testing their vocal apparatus and their wits and their fund of anecdotes against one another, you feel almost kindly toward your mother who told you to sit back in the corner and be still.

Listening to such groups, you feel, if you are a modest one, the strength that resides in deep water. But your greatest advantage — and it is a deadly advantage that the talkers seem never to be aware of — lies in the fact that nobody can talk more than an hour or two, to such an ear as yours, without giving a pretty fair revelation of himself. It doesn't matter how evasive he is, or how smart he thinks he is. As a matter of fact, the more evasive he is and the more he shines when thinking of himself the more quickly and appallingly he will come out. Knowing that, the modest person sits back, puts on a countenance that looks a bit ignorant and stupid, and waits for the revelations. For he will use these, in one way or another, if he is a novelist. And if he has the cunning that years of silence ought to have given him, he will, more by the way he looks than by anything he says, encourage the voluble ones to undress clear to their marrow. I confess without even a blush that I shamelessly encouraged Stephen Spender by giving him a smile or a chuckle in those appropriate moments that led him to think that I was bright enough to appreciate him.

It was Cabell, I believe, a misunderstood and grossly neglected writer, who once advised us to enter an empty auditorium and talk to the empty benches, if we would discover what we think. There may be no better way. When we talk to persons, we are seldom interested in what we think or believe, if indeed we are fortunate enough to have beliefs that rest on more than prejudice. We are intent on making a favorable impression on another mind. That we so rarely do argues that we say little and say it poorly, or that envy and frustration have made us an unreceptive people. When one goes into a chamber to speak to empty benches one is talking to himself; and one is seeking not applause but light. That may be one reason authors turn now and then to what is called autobiographical fiction.

60

The late Thomas Wolfe was certainly not a profound man, but his intuitions were sometimes luminous. I have always liked his statement that a person writes a book to forget it, though possibly he was not the first to say it. That was true of him and it seems to be true of those whose writing is called subjective. Some, like Wolfe, are never able to forget the story but in desperation write it over and over. Some, like Proust and Joyce, make personal catharsis the project of a lifetime.

We write stories to forget them and we talk to empty benches. That much in our motivation seems to be good. We also write the stories in an effort, through the purge of confession, to obliterate a sense of guilt and to redress old wrongs. That part of the motivation seems to be futile. The story cannot be forgotten until we come to terms with its materials, and we cannot come to terms merely by dramatizing it in a thousand pages. We are no less deluded, it seems to me, in other aspects of the motivation. The autobiographical novelist, because of having been turned outside in and made introverted, is likely to be pretentiously modest and self-effacing, and to write books with the hope of applause rather than understanding. What appears to be great courage may be little more than exhibitionism; he may seem to be honest, while striving at every turn to put the best face on himself.

All novels, it has been said many times, are autobiographical for those able to read. Only those are called autobiographical that make extensive use of obviously personal experiences. It is assumed that I have published such books. I had intended as early as 1925 to write the Vridar story but put it off, hoping for clearer perspective and motivations. I wanted irony to burn out the dross and shine in cold light on the pages, for I was resolved that the books would not be an exercise in self-idolatry. I have been told a thousand times that I went to the other extreme and made Vridar twice the imbecile he actually was. Thomas Wolfe has Eugene Gant in diapers exchanging winks with Voltaire, but to Vridar Hunter at the age of twenty I gave about half the sense of a ten-year-old child. I suspect that Wolfe and I both got off the track, and for the same reasons.

I intended my story to be a comedy in the Meredithian sense, in the sense of *The Egoist*, but was forced to admit that its humor was not that of the Comic Muse but of Jonathan Swift. Vridar's spiritual anguish, insane jealousies, nightmares of lunacy, and halfwitted flounderings right and left are all meaningless if not placed in perspective against a background of Mother, Father, Time, and the Earth. That reviewers on the whole found the books as humorless as a mausoleum and as unpleasant as an undernourished child I take to be the author's fault. The project should have been longer delayed.*

Still another matter in my playing the modest man has caused me years of regret. In a prefatory insert, I wrote, with tongue deep in cheek, that the protagonist was going to write an honest book. In those years I still overrated book reviewers. I had never for a moment thought that they would miss the satanic irony in that. They all missed it. Some, holding the offending statement up for an incredulous world to mock, said that all four novels were dishonest and pretentious. Others said the books were the only honest or in any case the most honest novels yet published. They were both wrong.

Surely any enlightened person must know that it is utterly impossible for anyone to write an honest book. The intention may be honest, though to determine that, we'd have to explore the author's unconscious mind. I cannot foresee the time when there will be, when there *can* be, an honest book. Before such a book can be written, homo sapiens will be so clearly understood that evasions, deceptions, and concealments will be too palpably silly to be practiced by anyone.

The reviewers, as well as the many Vridars who wrote me long letters, would have been more to the point if they had seen in the four novels neither honest nor dishonest books but a monumental wail from another of the modest and long-silent ones. I am aware that this kind of confession looks neurotic in a country where the most brazen and blatant self-promotion is looked on as a sign of genius. Nevertheless, in an enlightened country a critic of sharp insights might well have written, "Here are four tomes, of more than half a million words in the aggregate, by one who, bullied and almost castrated in his childhood, driven to the wailing walls in his

---

* The tetralogy has been rewritten and incorporated into novel 12 of the historical Testament of Man series.

adolescence, and delivered over to insanities in adulthood, has at last broken his schizoid silence in an interminable diarrhea of words, without parallel in those similarly afflicted. Ordinarily these anguished creatures are able to address themselves to the universe in one large volume, but Fisher's outburst has demanded four; and if the reticence of the man is measured by the vehemence of his style, we can expect that this one who was his mother's silent little man will assault our sensibilities for another fifty years. Let's not be astonished if his remembrance of things past overtakes, in volume at least, that of Proust . . ."

The silent and manly little one, for whom modesty had become a way of life, might indeed have gone on wailing if he had not fallen on Lewisohn's *Expression in America*. In that stimulating book is the observation that practically all American authors have gone to seed, and still go to seed, in early middle age. Lewisohn's reasons for this, if he gave any, I do not remember, but the dire admonition I took to heart. For one thing, of course, writers in this country are trademarked soon after they appear, and it is assumed that a Lewis, Dreiser, Dos Passos, Steinbeck, Hemingway, Faulkner, O'Hara, and many others can be recognized in any department store. That is true and possibly it should be true. For another thing, these shadows athwart the forlorn hope, confusing book reviewers with literary critics, fall into the self-destroying habit of trying to run true to their brand. In imitation of themselves they sometimes perish.

I felt that I was likely to follow in the footsteps of those who had gone before me, but that if I did it could not be said that I hadn't seen the handwriting on the wall. If we try to look above and beyond the trademarks that reviewers attach to our lapels, we may find ourselves adrift in shallow waters, with *Time's* book department as a compass; or we may, on the other hand, try, as Wolfe tried, to forget the books of our apprenticeship and find a larger field. If we do, modesty then will have been the parent of humility, and that kind of parent, no matter what his vices, we can forgive.

Comments on

His Testament of Man Series

". . . how thou wentest after me in the wilderness, in a
land that was not sown."

By the time I had completed the third volume of my tetralogy about
Vridar Hunter, I had reached the conclusion that most of the arts,
philosophy in general, and most of the writing about mankind, have
had as their unconcealed and unabashed purpose his glorification. In
nearly all of it the ugly, the brutal, the stupid, and the areas with
no apparent meaning, have been glossed and glamorized or ignored.
When someone tries to give a picture of the whole of it, he is called
a debunker or muckraker and is accepted only by the few who have
the courage and mind to demand the whole of it. I was at that time
reading widely in autobiography and autobiographical fiction and I
had found a few authors who had not looked steadily in a mirror
at the well-beloved. None, within my reading range, had indulged
in such fantastic self-glorification as Thomas Wolfe in his novel *Look
Homeward, Angel*.

I have written about this elsewhere, particularly the incredible
fourth chapter, and shall say here only as much as I need to say to

make a point. Wolfe and I had talked two or three times about the autobiographical novels we were working on, and it was, I am sure, after he learned that I intended to write three or four volumes that he decided to write more than one — though being the kind of person he was, he would have had to write more than one anyway. How did the two of us look at our protagonist? Wolfe has his baby Eugene still in diapers, unable to walk or talk, "but thinking quietly of many things before he dropped off to sleep." Instead of portraying the infant Vridar at the age of a year and a half as one heartsick with horror because he had emptied his bladder in his diaper; as one whose knowledge of the people around him was disillusioned and shrewd and adult; and as one who looked down the years and saw himself as a lonely misunderstood genius — instead of all that, I set Vridar before the reader as an ugly red mindless idiot of a thing, who didn't know he had a bladder, hadn't the faintest notion of language, much less a ravenous hunger for books, and didn't distinguish between his snickering relatives and the wallpaper.

H. G. Wells has told us that he "struggled with a considerable measure of success against the common vice of self-protective assumptions . . . I was seeing myself as far as possible without pretences, my *persona* was under constant scrutiny, even at the price of private and secret sessions of humiliation." I take this to mean that Wells was aware of man's tendency to lose all sight of self in the image that vanity creates. No doubt the author who would be popular does well to remain within the self-protective assumptions and to accept as an indispensable part of the human gospel what Ellen Glasgow called the illusion of disillusionment.

From the time of my earliest memories my *persona* was under my own constant scrutiny. Far from indicating while still in diapers a "ravenous hunger for pictures and print," and far from wondering savagely how my relatives would feel if they knew what I thought of them, I was, not even then but later, so cursed and borne down by a sense of being unworthy and meaningless and so defenseless in a brutal world that my struggle came to be less with self-protective assumptions than with people who were lost in them.

I do not say that there are not wonderful things in the Wolfe novel and I don't agree with Auden that it is no more than grandoise rubbish; but in my view Wolfe's books overglorify the infant, boy, man — who from birth is wretched, tortured, frenzied, not, we are asked to believe, because of imperfections in him but because of the nature of the people and the world around him. I resolved to have as little of that as possible. I had in mind a protagonist with a few virtues and a lot of faults and I was determined to put him before the reader for what he was. I surely was not able to do that, but I did bear down on his faults with such clear definitions that the late Joseph Henry Jackson publicly washed his hands of Vridar, the late William Rose Benet almost shrieked his distaste, and John Chamberlain hurled him through a window — in the manner, I have liked to believe, of Walter Savage Landor who, after pitching an offending book through a window, suddenly roared in a stricken voice, "My God, I forgot the violets!"

It would be foolish, in my opinion, to contend that Wolfe revealed Wolfe in Gant-Webber, or I Fisher in the early Vridar Hunter story, or Henry Adams Henry Adams, for that matter, in the education of Henry Adams. For one thing, no matter how honorable our purpose and firm our will, when we try to put aside the sham and pose, none of us would dare to step completely out of the self-protective assumptions and stand naked before a cynical world. I have never seen Shelley plain, or any other man. A critic has said in *The Humanist* that my latest version of Vridar "is perhaps the one modern novel of the artist as man in which he stands naked and unafraid." I am afraid that as he stands there he is neither.

For another thing our knowledge of our wellsprings is not yet deep enough to enable us to determine in all instances, or possibly in any, the line between assumption and fact. Dr. Victor Robinson hardly exaggerates when he says that "Intellectually, we are but a stone's throw from the Stone Age; emotionally, we are still living there." In the past fifty years many persons have in different ways expressed the same thought. Dr. Bronson Feldman in *The Unconscious in History* said it on another level: ". . . symbolism evolved specifically from the dream tendency of *displacement* — the unconscious mechanism that drains nervous intensity from an unpleasant image or theme, one which cannot bear consciousness, to imbue something else that can . . ." The matter is again put before us by V. Stefansson in *The Standardization of Error* when he says that errors widely and generally agreed upon are far more convenient than truth, because, as Dr. Wendell Johnson says, truth tends to change, whereas error "agreed upon and firmly fixed in legend and in law, is something one can count upon from day to day, even from century to century."

Before I had completed my four novels about Vridar, I was pretty sick of the task. There had been gathering in me a doubt so strong that it dismayed my intuitions and almost paralyzed my will. I could not for a while imagine why this was so; I could not believe that it was due to a failure of moral courage. I was forced at last to the conclusion that my doubts were based in a lack of knowledge. With this thought in mind, I decided to give a few years to exploratory reading in a number of fields.

The time came when I wrote my publisher that *Darkness and the Deep,* the first novel in a projected series, was offered as the introduction to a work-in-progress. I confessed to a feeling that the task was too big for me, and said that after many years of study I was approaching it experimentally. I thought that my efforts, in their final sum, would be no more than a piece of pioneering in a difficult field. I said that as long as the field lay fallow to the artist, writing fiction about the present, unless merely to entertain, seemed to me too much like trying to understand the adult without exploring his childhood.

Now that the task is completed, I feel, in looking back, that it was too big for me. I think that if a writer were to attempt what I attempted, his preparation should begin early and his education should be directed toward his goal. I started late, very late, and so abused my eyes and health and drove myself at a pace that only my wife was ever allowed to see, realizing more clearly as the years passed that I'd never be able to write as many novels for the series as I had hopd to write. Worse than that, I never had enough time to assimilate and reflect on the countless wonderful facts and implications in the learned articles and more than two thousand books that I read. I developed a case of chronic mental indigestion.

Here are instances of what I mean. Prof. Shotwell has written:

"There is no more momentous revolution in the history of thought than this, in which the achievements of thinkers and workers, of artists, philosophers, poets and statesmen, were given up for the revelation of prophets and a gospel of worldly renunciation." What a vista that opens! — and how many have ever seen it? How many of the apologists for Judaism and Christianity know how much the prophets and the renunciation have cost us?

On the wall facing me, when I sat at my desk, I put typed statements, so that I would see them in moments of contemplation. Shotwells' was there. Two from Bentwich were there — that the selection and separation of Israel was the constant theme of the Prophets, and that the war of the Maccabees against Jews who would Hellenize Israel and against Syria was the most fateful turning point in history for the Western world. What if the followers of the Prophets had lost that war? In that case there could never have developed what is called Christianity. To say that the world would be worse off if it had not developed is to make habit, tradition, and self-protective assumptions the supreme law of the mind.

In that panel was Sumner's statement, that the change from the mother family to the father family "is the greatest and most revolutionary in the history of civilization." What a realm that opens to speculation, when we bear in mind such facts as these, that the ancient Hebrews had no divine mother, and that their form of the father family more than anything else has shaped the Western world. But in the dozens of statements on the wall before me none opened a wider world to me and to none did I give more hours of thought than to Cumont's: "If the torrent of actions and reactions that carries us along were turned out of its course, what imagination could describe the unknown regions through which it would flow?"

Looking back across the past, at one fateful war of ideas and another, one must ask oneself, What would the world be like today if the torrent had flowed in another channel? What if Greek values had triumphed, and there had been no Juadism and Christianity based on the revelation of prophets and a gospel of renunciation of this life? We can only wonder about it; the torrent took the other channel, and here we are. Those who feel that the whole thing has been under divine guidance need not wonder at all.

In that panel was the observation that all languages today are little more than dictionaries of faded metaphors. That is not an exaggeration. Edward Carpenter asked, which of us has seen a tree? For primitive peoples a tree was a house of God, a phallic likeness, a miracle from the earth-womb, a living, breathing thing, with speech, powers, and spirit. One hardly knows whether to be more impressed by the richness of primitive man's language, or dismayed by the skeleton of it, stripped of flesh and spirit, which we use today.

* * *

After I had read in the records many years and had come to a fair notion of my ignorance, I wrote my publisher that Schulberg had not been able to tell us what made Sammy run, Wolfe had not known what made Gant-Webber run, and I had not known what made Vridar run. The matter, I had come to suspect, was not the simple one of the adult's childhood; it was the complex matter of his entire history, which is the history not only of mankind but of the whole plant and animal world. Writers may never be able to tell their readers what makes Sammy run, but after thirty years of reading about the past I knew more about Vridar (I said to my publisher) than I had known when I wrote his story.

Well, a little more anyway. It was a big step away from mankind's tacit agreement to accept errors as facts when I faced up to such matters as these, that moral values and conscience are in no sense innate but have to be acquired; that in our Western society hostility in some measure between father and son is inevitable; that Judaism and Christianity, for all their professed rapport with the supernatural, are largely an idealization of the family relationship, with nearly all the emphasis on the male side (where *is* the daughter?); that the refusal of the prophets to accept a divine mother (I still don't know and no man seems to know why) has produced a schizoid Western world. These are only three of a multitude of recognitions that were forced on me. How depressing to contemplate a patriarchy so inflexible and tyrannical, under the Hebrews, and for centuries under the Christians, that women were denied their rightful place! Margaret Mead has told us that those virtues and qualities peculiar to the female sex, or found in it in greater richness, played so little part, or no part at all, in shaping our values and institutions that the male's blindness to those qualities has been a great loss to all of us. You have to look no farther than to the ghastly wars in this century to believe that.

Some historians go to the past to write about wars and cæsars; some, about philosophers who lost themselves in mysticism; and a few go to write about ideas. My interest was more in symbols and myths and the standardization of errors. I have sometimes felt that Dr. Mortimer Adler and his brilliant staff have spent a lot of time on a little; most of the "great" ideas belong with the cartouche, the icon, and the cross. If the *Synopticon* were an index to the hungers and forces out of which the ideas came — yes, and of the distortions of reality, personality, and mind that helped to shape ideas — we might have a better idea of Sammy. But Plato and Augustine and Aquinas don't help us in that at all.

For years I read standard works in a number of fields; then studies of the primitive mind; and at last undertook a systematic course of intensive reading in comparative religions, archaeology, anthropology, not overlooking along the way such fields as music, medicine, geography, climate, customs — or even beverages and athletics. Now and then I thought I was catching a glimpse of Sammy and Eugene and Vridar away back there in the dim mists; and I began to feel a little more sanguine, to feel that I had a chance to discover a few of the hungers and fears and unreasons that had shaped them down through the centuries. I hoped to find the answer to some questions that had troubled me. Why, for instance, did most persons, indeed, all but a few persons, seem to be hostile to the unflattering facts of their history? Robinson Jeffers has said that men hate the truth, that they would rather meet a tiger on the road. The more I read and pondered the more I became convinced that facts are their best and strongest friends, and standardized errors their most deadly enemy. Did men hate truth because of deeply-buried feelings of guilt, because of inordinate self-love, because of ignorance or stupidity, or chiefly because of fear?

Someone has said that forcing the social organism to emerge from its primitive origins, covered over with its myths and legends, is like bringing a ship to the surface that has been sunk a long time. It does not seem to be a happy analogy. The myths and legends are a large part of the social organism we have today. Frazer put it well: "It is indeed a melancholy and in some respects thankless task to strike at the foundations of belief in which, as in a strong tower, the hopes and aspirations of humanity through long ages have sought refuge from the storm and stress of life. Yet sooner or later it is inevitable that the battery of the comparative method should breach these venerable walls, mantled over with the ivy and moss and wild flowers of a thousand tender and sacred associations. . . . The task of building up into fairer and more enduring forms the old structures so rudely shattered is reserved for other hands, perhaps for other and happier ages. We cannot foresee, we can hardly even guess, the new forms into which thought and society will run in the future. . . . Whatever comes of it, wherever it leads, we must follow the truth alone. It is our guiding star."

The rapid expansion of the frontiers of knowledge in the more exact sciences has forced agonized reappraisals not only of the social sciences but also of all religious and ethical systems. The totalitarian leaders propose to demolish the mantled towers with abrupt and violent revolution. The so-called open societies, confused, dismayed, and disintegrating, are trying to proceed by evolution but seem to have suffered a partial paralysis of will. It may take a long while yet before man perceives that the object in the road is not a tiger — that truth is a grace and a blessing, and that the chief enemy is the closed societies with their standardized errors, the self-protective assumptions, and the disease of self-idolatrous hostility to truth which fear and ignorance beget.

* * *

Three questions have been put to me more commonly than any others. How, living in Idaho ("— of all places!") did I get so many books to read; how did I determine who were the greatest authorities in various fields; and how did I know what novels I wanted to write? Let's take them in that order.

Some of the great libraries over the nation sent the books to my rural mailbox. If the Library of Congress did not have a book I wanted (many of them it did not have) the reference librarian gave me the name of one or more libraries that had the book. Now and then I left Idaho to read in large libraries. Two or three hundred of the most indispensable books I bought.

Discovering the ablest authorities in a social science field is not difficult: they are those held in the highest esteem by the greatest number of scholars in the field. Take for instance the Old or New Testament: if your interest is in the facts and probabilities, you will waste no time reading theologians. You would waste time if you were to read without guidance books about the Bible; there have been thousands of them, most of them based not on historical facts but on legend and tradition. You would wish to search the learned journals in a field, talk to a reference librarian when you found a good one, thumb through catalog files and indexes, observe which school, if any, the author is associated with, and keep a file. Once you get inside a field and are sure of a few of the greatest scholars, you will have no trouble finding your way.

In the New Testament it wouldn't take you long to learn that Bacon (to name one) is a giant; but here, as in any field close to Judaism or Christianity, you should move warily, with your wits about you. Streeter was a big name, too, but time and again you will find him shockingly pious and naive, as when he says that neither Peter nor any of the Twelve witnessed the sufferings of "Christ" — it has not been proved that there were twelve, or that there was a Peter, or that there was a Jesus of Nazareth. One of your chronic headaches will develop over the fact that a scholar can be so detached and sound when his prejudices are not touched, so childlike when they are.

There is Mommsen, whom one scholar has called the prince of scholars of the 19th century. He was a great scholar, certainly, but his uncritical admiration of Julius Caesar is a dreadful bore. Emotion has no legitimate place in scholarship, and adulterates it when present. Oesterley and Robinson are among the Higher Critics of the Old Testament, and, so far as I know, are sound there; but they are simply not scholars when they come to the New. The ablest Jewish scholars, such as Montefiore, Hirsch, and Loewe, can be detached in the New Testament but not in the Old. Even Frazer, who has few peers, was not himself when he wrote about such subjects as Jesus. Are there any who never slipped? Only a few, so far as

I was able to tell — Cumont, at least in his books that I read, and Henry Charles Lea in all his work. Considering his background, Loisy did nobly. Reading hundreds of scholars in a lot of fields one is immensely delighted when they rise into the clear light that shines above all indoctrination, and distressed and dismayed when they sink back into the primitive gloom. There is a piety gathered at the knee of mother or church that all but a few men seem unable to rise above.

How did I know what books I wanted to write? In the beginning I did not know. As a graduate student, and during my years as a teacher, I ranged widely in the past, guided by no purpose but love of knowledge; I knew my way around there only as one knows his way around Europe who in two or three months has tried to see the principal things. One returns to Europe again and again, if one wishes to know it well, and it is this way with the past: on the first journey you get some kind of notion of London, Paris, Rome, Madrid; on the second you discover more of their treasures and reach out to other places; on the third or fourth you may explore the simplicities of peasant life.

Discovering the past has been like that for me. The temperament of the scholar is a thing of its own. It is wonderfully exciting after years of work to find yourself more and more in possession of a field. I have never possessed any field; it takes a lifetime and a major talent to become the leading authority in even a small area; I have ranged over too many fields to be the master of any, but I have gone deep enough in a few, such as the time of Solomon or the Roman world in the first century, to have a fair idea of the scholar's dedication, and of the intellectual and spiritual enrichment that comes from being well-established in a province of one's choosing.

I knew from the first that I'd want to write a novel about the ape-man. I think I was not half as successful as I had wished to be, in projecting myself into the small dim world of those stooped, short-legged, hairy ancestors, who were learning to walk in an upright position and to convert their front feet into hands. The second novel, with its theme (a magnificent one) of the ghost and the grave, satisfies me no more; nor the third, with its attempt to adumbrate various female qualities, which an evolving and triumphant patriarchy forced into perversions of their natural goodness; nor the fourth, with

73

its intimations and forecasts of those distortions of the male psyche that are so obvious a part of the modern world. I felt that I was more successful in the fifth — with the emergence of the Son and the Castrate, for in a sense I had been both. All the while I made attempts, of course, to show different faces of the emerging Male and Female, Adam and Eve, Father and Mother, as well as to suggest if not the origin at least early phases in the development of various ideas and forces, myths and distortions, in our modern world.

A writer in the Western world who undertakes such a series would know from the first that he would have to write about the ancient Hebrews, the later Jews, and the Christians. In the prehistoric era, the matters are pretty dark: what were the essential things then, that made a heel of Sammy, a hulking self-beloved of Eugene, a frightened schizoid of Vridar? Was there any meaning deeper than the dismal and desperate effort to hide the ghost under the tombstone? Was worship of the sexual function the heart of the soul? Those long-ago times have bequeathed to us a few crude drawings and tools, but we know only a little about the human psyche in prehistoric times. Before the so-called dawn of history, the human male emerged triumphant in the social scheme, war became a divine instrument, the Son-symbol began its long climb to pre-eminence, and the daughter sank below the consciousness of even the major poets. In the Western world there are few more biting ironies than the fact that the Son has been glorified in every conceivable way, whereas the Daughter is still only the daughter, un-ennobled and unsung.

In what is called the historic era, the writer interested in what makes Sammy run and not in costume-and-dagger tales for uncritical readers will find many more great themes than he will have time for. He may, like me, pass up the great pharaoh Akhnaton and his time, which saw the clear emergence of monotheism and the concept of a more compassionate deity — that is, of a patriarchy with its ferocity slightly softened. Keeping his eye on Sammy and Eugene and Vridar, he will not dare pass up that long and crucial struggle between the kings and the prophets — between the figtree and the desert, the vallys of vision (and fruitfulness) and the mounts of Sinai (and celibacy). If he writes about that struggle (the prophets won) whose results went so deep into the millions of Vridars and

Eugenes, he will touch extremely sensitive nerves in those looking at the tiger on the road. He can expect to be ignored or smeared. It would be quite otherwise if he threw all the scholars out and put on Solomon's tongue a lot of things he never said and had no power to conceive of, such as the Song and the Proverbs.

For a while the great Captivity was in my plan, for I wished to strip it of its accretions of legend and myth; but in Vridar's psyche, this dispersal of a people seemed not to be of the first importance. The extremely bitter struggle between Jews who wanted to hellenize Israel and those who wanted to preserve it in racial and religious isolation — the struggle between beauty and righteousness — *was* of transcendent importance: obsessed by fear of the wifeless and womanless Father, allergic to women and to practically all pleasures, the lean, shaggy, angry prophets won a second time. The price the Eugenes and Vridars paid for that victory no one, so far as I know, has ever tried to determine.

Whether or not I looked like a tiger on the road, I don't know, but my novel about Solomon led most of the "Jewish" critics to wash their hands of me. By the time I began to write about what some people call the Christian era, most reviewers had had enough of me. That of course was their privilege. I had no quarrel with their interpretation of the Jesus or any other symbol, but I do feel that my side, on which are so many of the world's greatest men and women, has a right to be heard. Long ago it should have been said that when all the facts are in, the truth of any matter turns out to be greater, and usually far greater, than any of its explanations to be found in myth, legend, and tradition. This is because the myth-makers have had so little knowledge to stand on. If those who believe in "God" look for proof, I suggest that that fact would stand exploration.

My novel about Jesus I called a parable; it is a novel of estrangement, of the immolation of the Son. The story concludes with these words: "No, not that. Don't you see that he has come again? Can't you understand it now? He has come in the only way he will ever come — as he came a hundred or a thousand years ago; as he will come again next year, or a hundred or a thousand years from now.

Don't you see? He has come, he will come again, he will keep coming, until in this world there are no more Lucias hunting for their lost children, no more soldiers with lances by dead men in the night. . . ."

For what can the great truth of it be? — except the struggle of conscience to become more than a spark in a few breasts? — to become a flame, a torch, a light, until there can be no more Hitlers, Stalins, Mussolinis — and (I for one hope) no more Sammys and Eugenes and Vridars.

The traditional story of early Christianity and its origins let those think a great story who must; I think the true, the historically factual, story is a thousand times greater. I think it one of the great stories of human history. I have tried to tell it in A Goat for Azazel, a novel of Christian origins and of transfiguration. The distaste and horror with which some readers have viewed my story compels one to wonder how long man will persist in measuring himself by the usually false, often childish, and sometimes evil explanations of the primitive or the ancient mind. After more than thirty years studying his record, I can tell you this, that the truth and the facts flatter him more than the myths and fantasies which he has spun out of ignorance and fear. The traditional and accepted story of Christianity's origins and emergence is an insult to man's mind and spirit, when compared to the astonishing creative act, in both selectivity and synthesis, of the actual inception and growth. The true story is as much greater than the story which Christians revere as the scope and complexity of this universe is greater than the primitive concept of its origin and nature as set forth in Genesis.

Certain people, clinging in fear to old forms, obsolete ideas, and closed systems, have called me a misanthrope. Others have called me a cynic and atheist. They should have gone back with me. I spent many years back there, and all along the way found evidence not only of man's grievous errors and infinite capacity to make a fool or a brute of himself, but also of his potential for growth and greatness. My view of Solomon (who in my novel is of course a symbol) put a firmer structure under hope and faith than the childlike notion of him as the epitomist of all wisdom. The view of Jesus as a virgin's son who bore a cross and died for the sins of men seems to me unspeakably unworthy of man at his noblest reach, and far inferior to my representation of the symbol as that golden nimbus of love and compassion that is to be seen shining now and then — especially after an orgy of Belsens and Katyn Forests, where man is found debased far below the level of the beasts, not because he is by nature lower but because of the perversions and distortions which fear and ignorance have wreaked upon his soul.

In the Foreword of my concluding novel, *Orphans in Gethsemane,* I put it this way: "I stand on this, that if man is ever to build a civilization worthy of that devotion which he seems richly endowed to give, he will first have to accept in the full light of his mind and soul the historical facts of his past, and the mutilations and perversions which his hostility to these facts has made upon his spirit. Only in the forces, ideas, and traditions that have produced him, and are the essence of his being, can man find his sanctions and powers; but we must hope that he need not forever cherish, because of fear and ignorance, the atavisms in these forces, ideas, and traditions, or continue to be so much an expression of their will, once the necessity in their origins is understood and respected."

Not the good or the evil but the necessity, for reasons still obscure to us. It was precisely these perversions and distortions which hostility to fact had made upon their spirit that sent thousands of men fleeing into the African desert, to torture and debase their flesh and minds in an effort to elevate their souls; or that caused other men to put millions of their fellows to torture, dungeons, and flame. From that time in the remote past when my character Yescha unmanned himself and flung his testicles as a peace-offering to the Sun-Father, to that dark and unholy hour when Hitler shrank back into the bitter lie of his being and swallowed cyanide, man has been making a hideous thing of his emotions, because his mind has seen no farther than his hands could reach. Now and then his obscene alliance with brutality and murder has been illuminated, momentarily, by a revelation of his potential for compassion and fellowship. It is in these few precious moments that Jesus comes again.

But I can see no Jesus, no light, no radiance in doctrines of human depravity and original sin: in these, men are kneeling in the catacombs of primitive ideas. This surrender of spirit to the past is a plain unwillingness to leave the hospital. One who spends most of a lifetime exploring and searching that past, for the full measure of its many horrible and few lovely things, knows that the only direction in which the healthy mind can look is ahead. Such doctrines as original sin are a hospital, and the only people there are sick people who don't want to get well.

Out of infinite darkness we come and we return to infinite darkness, each of us a spark of something in an infinitesimal moment. "Whatever comes of it, wherever it leads, we must follow the truth alone. It is our guiding star." When man learns that it is also his friend and his only friend, he may achieve greatness in the wide realms of his spirit, with that genius and daring with which he now achieves in the realm of his mind.

The Novelist and His Background

When it was suggested that I should take as my topic this evening "The Novelist and his Background," I felt dismay, even though it may be supposed that serious writers know something about the subject. Mention of "serious" writers invariably brings to my mind the story of that tedious congressman who, after wearying his colleagues with a long-winded speech, turned to Henry Clay and said, "You, sir, speak for the present generation but I speak for posterity." Clay, you will remember, said to him, "You seem resolved to speak until the arrival of your audience." All serious writers like to believe, with the congressman, that they speak for posterity; but as we approach old age we understand more and more clearly that we do well indeed if we speak for ourselves.

I felt dismay at the thought of talking to this group because I am not in any special sense of the word a folklorist. Still, any writer, I suppose, is a folklorist, or any artist of any kind. My dictionary says that folklore is the customs and beliefs of a people or a study

* A talk given to the Western Folklore Conference and to the Writers' Workshop at Denver, July 17, 1953.

of them. In that sense folklore is as broad as human life itself, and a novelist's materials are surely a part of it. In a narrower sense, folklore is myth. Myth, any myth, it has been said, is an effort to explain a custom or belief whose origins have been forgotten, or, more likely, were never known. Myth, it may be, is the more spacious formula in which the lore is contained; and myth, I understand after so many years of writing, is the chief thing in a novelist's background.

I do not know how well this matter is understood by people generally. Many years ago when I was a college teacher I was called on the carpet by an angry president, who was tired of hearing complaints about me from parents, the alumni, and the board of regents. Pacing back and forth while wondering whether to fire me or reform me, he suddenly turned and asked, "Fisher, what in the devil do economics, sociology, psychology, and all these things have to do with courses in writing?" If a university president can be so limited in his view, we hardly dare suppose that there is much comprehension of the way folklore and myth and their wealth of symbols fill and overflow our lives.

In his book on Thomas Wolfe, Mr. Herbert Muller says that Wolfe tried to create the American myth. That statement startled me. Recently, when looking over the first issue of the Denver *Faulkner Studies*, I was again startled, when I found this author called an epic mythmaker. How, asked the critic, is one to understand Faulkner the mythmaker? It seems to me that here we have confused thinking. No man creates a myth. All myth is a product of the folkmind. It may be true that Wolfe was trying to represent what he conceived to be the American myth; and it may be that Faulkner is trying to search out the substance and color of ancient myth in the American South. But an effort to perceive in what ways myth shapes and determines life today is quite different from creating the myth itself.

Freud, toward whom in some quarters it is now the fashion to be indulgent, thought that myth "corresponds to the displaced residues of wish fantasies of entire nations." Otto Rank conceives of myth as an intermediate between collective dreams and collective poems. As the dream draws off the subconscious repressed emotion, so does the myth, creating for itself a "collective symptom for taking up all repressed emotion." Which, in both Freud and Rank, is another way of saying that if our reach does not exceed our grasp, what's a heaven for? It is another way of saying that emotion will create for human yearning those goals which mind cannot establish as fact. For according to Stucken, all myths are creation myths.

For Mr. Muller, myth is "not a way of disguising or evading the shocking facts of life but a way of ordering and accepting them." In accepting the shocking facts they are, of course, disguised. Muller goes so far as to suggest that all literature, philosophy, religion, yes, and even science, is mythology. It would be a great comfort at the moment to know that the atom bomb is a myth. Thomas Mann thinks that the mythical is "the pious formula into which life flows when it reproduces its traits out of the unconscious." I see no reason to call the formula pious, unless Mann intended to imply that the creative act is untouched by irony or doubt.

All these definitions we need not press too far. It may be that we do not quite know what myth is, for the reason that we have not been able satisfactorily to explore the unconscious mind. The mystic, who depends so much more on that mind than most of us, or who in any case makes fuller use of it, is still a riddle. Freud admitted that research in the concepts of folk psychology — that is, myths, sagas, and fairy stories — had not by any means been concluded; and though research has revealed a good deal since his death, we still walk in the dark with dim lanterns.

We can, of course, observe myth-making all around us. We can, that is, observe the creation of legend, which myth absorbs. In 1922 Professor James Weber Linn said to a group of us at the University of Chicago, "I felt like a lion in a den of Daniels." He claimed the witticism as his own, though it was old before he was born. In the *Reader's Digest* for March, 1950, Herbert Corey solemnly attributes the witticism to Willmot Lewis and gravely informs us that since Lewis first said it in 1931, it had enlivened the orations of hundreds of speakers. In such manner people build up their heroes. In some such manner, we may assume, myth is born. The stature of demigods all around us rises in legend, the embellishments of which will coalesce eventually to make the myth, which will become a part of biographies yet to be written.

As I see it, the chief task of the novelist is sufficiently to liberate himself from his background to be able to see it in fairly clear perspective. That he was unable to do this up to the time of his death was the tragedy of Thomas Wolfe. He was so enmeshed, so suffocated, so much the captive of all the forces that had made him, that he actually could place himself, as in *Look Homeward, Angel,* as a diapered babe, still unable to walk or talk, in the position of a sardonic and matured adult. In varying degrees we are all guilty; and we are guilty because the lore and myths of our world enfold and imprison us, embellishing what we take to be meanings, and enhancing our pitifully small egos. We have in some manner to break free, without on the one hand losing touch with the stuff that made us, without on the other mistaking our self-protective illusions for truths. The threat of a deeper and deeper schizophrenia broods over the struggle.

A novelist's background, it seems to me, is to be found less in the physical accidents of his life — in parents, neighbors, and geography — than in the past which produced the child. Many years ago a novelist published a story called *What Makes Sammy Run.* Sammy was a Hollywood heel, and in an effort to understand what had made him a heel, his creator went back to Sammy's childhood. But Schulberg never found out what made Sammy run, any more than in a later effort he found out what made Fitzgerald run. I had just read this novel when I said to my friend, Prof. Don MacRae, that it would be interesting to do the same job for some college professor — not that I intended to imply that all, or even most, college professors are heels. MacRae almost at once set himself to the task. The result was his Houghton Mifflin Fellowship novel, *Dwight Craig.* But I don't feel that MacRae was able to tell us what made Dwight Craig run. Some of you may be aware that I once rather exhaustively explored a man's childhood, with the hope of explaining how he came to be what he was. I also was unsuccessful, and the sense of my failure grew with me down the years.

Those who try to find the man in the child are unsuccessful because the man is not there. The man is in all the centuries of our past. One of Faulkner's critics says that in a Faulkner story everything has been said that it is necessary to say about the part of today that yesterday is. How wonderful if that were true! For if that were true we could now say what makes Sammy run. It would mean that we could talk quite precisely about the novelist and his background. In the midway of this our mortal life, wrote Dante, I found myself in a dark wood, astray. It would mean that we had come out of that dark wood. No man knows, says a line of poetry, through what wild centuries roves back the rose. It would mean that we would know the rose all the way back. In plain truth, we do not. Not even Faulkner, who so long and faithfully has explored these matters, knows that. Understanding what is necessary to say about the part of today that yesterday is is exactly the novelist's task. It is a task that still defeats us.

More than twenty years ago I realized that I had not been able to explain the man in terms of the child. I became aware that the author of *The Red and the Black*, great modern that he was, and so unflinching in his devotion to truth, had not explained Julien. I fell into such a fit of depression — in psychological jargon, into such a sense of frustration and failure — that I must have been in the condition of the man who, despairing of his sanity, went to see a psychiatrist. What he needed, the psychiatrist told him, was to get out and away from himself. The great comedian Grimaldi was in town; why didn't he go hear him and laugh and forget his troubles? And the poor miserable wretch replied, "Great God, *I* am Grimaldi!"

After some months of despair, devoid, I'm afraid, of the saving grace of irony, I came to the conclusion that to be able to explain what makes Sammy and all the rest of us run we must go to the past — which means, simply, that we must explore and try to understand the folk mind, and all the myths and symbols it has produced. For an exploration of that vast field one lifetime would never be enough. It is not only that we haven't the time; it is also that we know too little about the marvelous variety and richness of the symbols which the folk mind has evolved, and which still shape and direct all of us in ways that we never suspect. All the savagery of the past, said the great James George Frazer, lies so close to our surface that it constitutes a standing menace to us and our civilization. Proof of that we seem to have had in abundance in our time.

Perhaps without impropriety I may tell you that in the past

twenty-five years I have read about two thousand learned books about the past, in those fields most closely related to the novelist's background. If I had the time and the eyes to read another twenty-five years, I think I should be right where Grimaldi was when he sought help. I have learned a few things about the evolution of myth; I have stood aghast before the thousands of symbols whose meanings are now a matter of record; but chiefly I have merely opened a window on a tremendous vista which I shall have neither the time nor the mind to penetrate.

I may then be pardoned a touch of annoyance when I read that in a Faulkner story everything about the past has been revealed which is today relevant to the present. Mr. Faulkner, I am sure, must have been amused if he read that statement. He also has been exploring myth and symbol, and with an ingenuity which none of his contemporaries seems to possess, he has been manifesting the past in the present. Another Faulkner critic has said that one of his stories may be compared to the transition from the pagan to the Christian era. I do not know if Faulkner so intended it, but there was no such transition. Nineteen centuries of Christianity have done no more than to elaborate on and in some instances to refine ancient myths. I raise this point only to suggest that the knowledge of the best of us is still so inadequate that in almost no matter can we be sure that we do not err.

I have stated it as my view that the principal part of a writer's background is the myths that have shaped him. There is a luminous statement in Harold Bayley's two-volume *The Lost Language of Symbolism*: "Little or no distinction can be drawn between classic myth and popular fairy-tale: myth was obviously once fairy-tale, and what is often supposed to be mere fairy-tale proves in many instances to be unsuspected theology." This field is so vast that we have time to look at only one instance. The principal myth of the Western world is not God or the Mother but what we call the Christ; that is, the myth, found with practically all ancient peoples, of the deliverer, the savior, and with all but Jews, the sacrificial offering on the fructifying tree. The wealth of folklore, drawn from so many sources, that went into the making of this symbol is one of the marvels of human history. The tenacity with which the Western world has clung to this symbol suggests its depth in human yearning.

From a great many I choose this myth-symbol with the hope that it will indicate the scope of our problem, as well as its difficulties. We are all aware of that need in mankind for heroes, which Carlyle expressed so well. Heroes we possibly must always have, of some sort, which means only symbols to which we aspire — or if we do not aspire, being too indolent, symbols that can serve as points of reference, and as moral and spiritual nourishment. When hero-worship, so strong in the Greeks, was combined with the sacrificial scapegoat, which also was commonplace in the lore of the ancient world, mankind got its symbol of the savior — and in the process brought women to that degraded level the record of which is one of the most repulsive chapters in human history. We must understand the myth and its sources before we can understand the modern Western woman, or even, one is tempted to add, the sensational appeal of Mickey Spillane.

Today, Professor Richard W. Boynton has said in a recent book, we are beyond mythology, or should be. Possibly we should be but we certainly are not. It is not clear that we should be, for the reason that myth has always been the vehicle for what in any generation passes for truth. In regard to the Christ symbol, see what form it is taking today! We all know that the Christian churches are fighting for their lives. We all know that there is a force abroad in the world that passes loosely under the name of Communism. We all know that this force has had an extraordinary appeal to a great number of intellectuals; and though I have steadily resisted it, and for seventeen years have been publicly speaking out against it, I was forced to face some unpleasant realities before I turned away from that dark wood. That so many have been, and are still being, disillusioned in this new force, which some have called a religion, is of no interest to us this evening, save as we must wonder what direction the myth will now take.

The thing called Communism — it is not, of course, Communism at all — is, as well as I can make it out, a revival on the one hand of ancient emperor worship, which served the Caesars so well, and on the other an invasion, for its dupes if not for its exploiters, of the great spiritual vacuum being left by the slow withdrawal of Christianity. Boynton thinks the Christian churches should scrap their antiquated dogmas and replace them with a religion of human values. In short, he would abandon the myth. But myth will not be abandoned, and the hunger for heroes will not be put aside.

What we have then, as I see it, is a return to unabashed hero-worship, during this fateful time when an immanent and personal deity is being dethroned. Many people call that godlessness, but it may not be that at all. It can hardly be that as long as the myth is vigorous. That it is vigorous is established by the obvious facts, not only that so many persons tend to deify their political leaders, including the late Mr. Roosevelt, but also that a cradle-to-the-grave security, which the political messiahs promise, is taking the place of the older belief in a life after death. The political messiah is replacing the ecclesiastic, and the "emergency" is replacing hell.

We are today witnesses to this shift in the direction of an ancient myth. All things are yours, Paul told the simple folk who were the early Christians. Under the Christian myth all things were theirs in a life to come, in which inequities would be no more and wrongs would be redressed. As Professor Shotwell has said, "There is no more momentous revolution in the history of thought than this, in which the achievements of thinkers and workers, of artists, philosophers, poets and statesmen, were given up for the revelation of prophets and a gospel of worldly renunciation." That gospel of renunciation, the reward of which is a higher glory in another life, has been the very heart of the Christian myth.

Our conflict today is between that gospel, struggling to survive but inevitably doomed to extinction, and the gospel of the blessed and abundant life here and now. The myth has veered and changed color, but it is the same myth. God, again as remote and lost as that symbol was in the time of Jesus, when the symbol of his Son came down to restore the divine intimacy, now finds his attributes taken from the ecclesiastic and invested in the politician. It is tempting to speculate on the development of the myth in the years ahead; to inquire how long it will survive and what purpose it will serve; and to wonder if disillusionment in the myth's new form will be greater than in its old. All that lies beyond us tonight, but we should note

86

in passing that certain eminent writers, who loathe the form the myth is taking, have fled the scene, and sought a haven in a moribund Church. Mr. T. S. Eliot has said that a rational civilization will never work; to which, I should think, it is enough to retort that we can never know until we try it.

Now all this is surely an important part of a writer's background in a time of stress and change. It may well be that we apprehend only dimly, if at all. Novelists of a later age — if the novel as an art form survives, which is doubtful — will understand far better than we what makes Sammy run. Today, those who strive to understand are able to see, in broad but dim perspective, the outlines of some of the ancient forces which have shaped us. There are many important myths, an exploration of which might well constitute the highest form of intellectual adventure. Sometimes, it is true, we weary in this struggle to look inside the riddle; and though we may not walk out into the sea, as Virginia Woolf did, or jump off a ship into an ocean at midnight, as Hart Crane did, we do feel the need to shut out the past, which presses with such intolerable insistence upon the present.

In such moments we feel as William James felt about his guests. "Are we never," he impatiently asked his wife, "are we never to have an evening alone? Must I see people every night?" His faithful wife replied, "I shall see that nobody bothers you this evening." But at the first sound of the doorbell William was there, behind his wife, looking over her head and exclaiming with delight, "Come in! Do come right in!" And so it is with us, caught between these persistent guests from the past, whose presence wearies us, and the need to press on and re-establish our kinship with all things.

I have mentioned only one myth among many that are a part of the novelist's background, and of the background of all of us. It has been said that all fiction is autobiographical, and that of course is true. Of autobiography, Professor Boynton says that it "may be somewhat cynically described as the art of informing the world in print what you wish you had been, instead of giving it a portrait of what your enemies and hostile critics said you were." Our hostile critics usually manage to have their say. It is true, nevertheless, that not much fiction, past or present, can stand the scrutiny of enlightened minds. To build it strong and true enough to stand that scrutiny becomes more and more the duty imposed upon us. It is the great achievement of Stendhal, whom a critic as eminent as Taine read fifty or a hundred times, that he wrote strong and true for his day; and though the most famous literary critics of his time rejected him, and his contemporaries refused to read him, we are proud today to place him high above his enemies. For his intuitive anticipation of certain psychological truths are now commonplace.

I might have talked to you of more immediate matters in a novelist's background — of the clues which he must try to find — the clues to his nature and problems. But those clues, it seems to me, all lead back to more remote times, whether they be clues to his emotional hermaphroditism, or to his schizophrenia, or to the multitude of symbols in his dreams. They are clues that go back to Job's question, and to Pilate's, both of which remain unanswered. They are clues that go back to the ages, out of which came the stuff that makes today's child. We have gained so much in knowledge while losing so much out of memory. I am fond of Jean Paul's profound observation that language is a dictionary of faded metaphors. How true that is, any standard work on symbolism will reveal. Which of us, asked Edward Carpenter, has ever seen a tree? Not one of us has. For ancient peoples a tree was a house of God, a phallic symbol, a miracle standing in the earth-womb, an act of divine creation, a living breathing thing with speech, powers, and spirit. If we cannot see a tree, we have strayed a long way from the wisdom of the ancients. We must suspect that a great deal remains to be refound and a great deal to unlearn, before we can see Shelley plain. "All I have written and published," said Goethe, "are but fragments of a confession." We have only fragments still.

But as we explore, as we become more familiar with the knowledge which thousands of obscure scholars have put before us; as we understand with Joubert that a man of imagination without learning has wings but no feet; as we make knowledge serve our intuitive insights, and our insights feed more on knowledge and less on caprice — we shall add more and more to the great confession which is the history of the human race. We shall lose our self-protective illusions; we shall have to abandon one comforting myth after another; but we need never lose the deep truth which Emerson saw:

> 'Tis not in the high stars alone,
> Nor in the redbreast's mellow tone,
> But in the mud and scum of things,
> There always, always something sings!

The Novelist and His Characters

The story-teller is often asked, Are the people in your books those you have known or did you invent them? Some of us are asked, Are your stories autobiographical? In a country where the shyster lawyers are eager to sue anybody, authors often try to protect themselves with the words, Any resemblance to persons living or dead is purely coincidental. There must be resemblances, if book characters are human beings. After observing an "increasing habit among readers of finding themselves portrayed in every novel, and of being annoyed or unduly pleased," Sinclair Lewis introduced his *Bethel Merriday* with typical Lewis sarcasm. He concluded with the words, "But the happy days were with *Elmer Gantry* when, on the same Sunday morning, in the same western city, each of two clergymen announced from his pulpit that the Reverend Elmer had been drawn solely from him, but that the portrait was crooked.

"I shall merely point out," Lewis wrote, "that there is a tradition that fiction characters have to be called something. Of course writers might call them X76-4 or Pi R Square. But if we did, all

* A talk given to the Idaho Writers League Sept. 23, 1961, and to the Utah Writers League Sept. 8, 1962.

the persons with automobile licenses numbered X76-4 and all the coolies named Pi Lung Squong would write us, which heaven forbid." I have had my share of persons who wrote to say that inasmuch as there is only one family in the country named Bridwell, I must have based *Dark Bridwell* on it, or inasmuch as there is no known instance of a Weeg family in Idaho I obviously based June Weeg on June Weeg in Turtle Creek, Pennsylvania. As for the autobiographical novel, let's say that all tales are autobiographical in the sense that authors have nothing to write about except their own experiences and fantasies. Let us suppose that they may put persons in books in the sense that they may consciously or unconsciously use things they have observed in them or have heard about them. But in a deeper sense the characters of artists in books and plays are little more than projections of themselves into human types.

There once came to me a dear lady-writer who told me she had just read my book *The Erotic Nightingale*. That little book, which had a good title and not much else, I called *The Neurotic Nightingale*. This woman, with all the wonderful things hidden in her subconscious mind, would have blushed a rosy red all over if she had known what she revealed. One of my former college professors introduced me at a luncheon. He told the assembled people, more interested in the odors from the kitchen than in listening to me, that my first book was *The Imaginary Sonnets to a Madonna*. I think no one has ever seen or read an imaginary sonnet. My book was called *Sonnets to an Imaginary Madonna*. Now suppose I had written a novel in which a woman writer spoke those words to an author, and a professor those words about one of the author's titles; and suppose they had then written me to say I had put them in my book and they were going to sue me. Are we novelists supposed to write out of our hats?

Take for a moment the other question. It has been said by various critics that all of Thomas Wolfe's books are about himself. Do they ask us to believe that the scene is about Thomas Wolfe, where the infant Eugene Gant, bathed, powdered, diapered, and nursed, is lying in his crib and thinking what a hell of a thing it is that he can't control his bowels and bladder? — thinking that he was "heartsick with weary horror as he thought of the discomfort, weakness, dumbness, the infinite misunderstanding he would have to endure" before he was able to walk? — feeling a ravenous hunger for books? — wondering "savagely" what his brothers and sisters would feel if they knew what he thought about them? — seeing his life "down the solemn vista of a forest aisle"? — understanding "that men were forever strangers to one another, that no one ever really comes to know anyone. Never, never, never, never, never. His brain went black with terror" and "he heard a great bell ringing faintly, as if it sounded undersea. . . ."

Countless readers, including reviewers, literary critics, and Maxwell Perkins, his editor, seem to have found that scene entirely plausible, though for the person looking at the realities it is a fantastic piece of self-glorification. Are we going to say that Wolfe put Wolfe in that scene? Wolfe never put himself in books. What he put in books was a glorified sad lost misunderstood genius that he thought was Wolfe. It is not at all certain that any writer can put anyone in a book. We can project ourselves into types, and I wish to suggest to you how one of us tries to do it.

A look at actors may help us to understand the matter. I mean actors and not the late Gable and Cooper, or the present Brando and Taylor. These are not really actors; they have no power to be anybody but themselves. An actor is not a person who is merely himself in different roles. An actor is a person who can project himself into different personality types. Try to imagine, for instance, the shy withdrawn frightened schizoid trying to enter the emotions and soul of the exuberant outgoing extravert who is forever selling himself. Or the other way around. No enlightened person would pretend that Clark Gable could have convincingly played Hamlet, or nine-tenths of the Hollywood actresses Elizabeth Barrett or Emily Dickinson.

Most of the Hollywood people are comparable to the creators of stories for the mass audience — such stories, for instance, as appear in the journals for women. The people in such fiction have the simplest dimensions; their interests, tastes, and thoughts are those of the millions of simple people who like to read about them. They think in uncomplex terms and on superficial levels and they think with their emotions, in conformity with what is thought to be intelligent and proper by all the status-seekers. One with a talent for such writing doesn't have to project himself into various personality types. He needs only to shift his plots a little and change the names. It is a long way into depth from such a world to the world occupied by those writers who are deadly serious, and who sometimes are so serious that they are deadly. It is a few light-years between a Sloan Wilson and a Proust, a Grace Metalious and a Kafka, a Salinger and a James Joyce.

I do not speak as one critical of those who write for the mass-audience. *Exodus, Advise and Consent,* and all books like them are not art but propaganda, and must have a legitimate place in a world where so few people are interested in art. One way to measure the difference between the two points of view and positions I am trying to suggest is to take the Oscar Williams treasury of lyrics and compare the faces in the last pages with the faces of those who write popular fiction. Those in the Williams book, male and female, are emotionally immature unhappy children, who at various depths are artists; whereas the others look more adult, are more adult, and a thousand times more prosperous. With such talent as they have, these latter write for the millions, beget children, join clubs, worry over big income taxes, and die acclaimed and respectable. The others, the artists, are likely to jump off ships at midnight, as Hart Crane did; or wade into a river and drown themselves, as Virginia Woolf did; or get drunk and choke to death in their vomit, as a poet recently did; or become chronic alcoholics, as Fitzgerald, Dylan Thomas, Sinclair Lewis, and so many others have done; or go insane with Ezra Pound, Swift, and many more; or run away from their mates, which seems to be the commonest and gentlest way of all.

If you have read about artists in different fields you know that they don't present a pretty picture — not even such saintly persons as Wordsworth, Tennyson, and Dickens. But we must remember that the artist is a child to the day of his death. How preposterous it would be to argue that Modigliani, Toulouse-Lautrec, and Utrillo were adult — or such as Chopin and Stravinsky, Shelley and Swinburne — or even Beethoven and Wagner, Thomas Hardy and Henry James. Persons who feel impatiently that artists should grow up and swear no more than Baptists, drink no more than Mormons, and kneel on holy days before what passes in some quarters as the eternal verities simply don't know what art comes from. If they don't think art is worth what it costs, they should stop being bothered by it, for there are enough summer places and men in gray flannel to take up their time.

A story is told of a certain child-author whose thoughts were always on himself and his books. One night after talking for hours about his own affairs, it occurred to him that it would be a nice thing to let his friend have a word or two. So, magnanimously, he said, "Look, I've been doing most of the talking. You talk. Tell me about yourself." "What about myself?" asked the weary friend. "Oh, anything — what you think about my books, for instance." It has been said of Proust that he so loved the sound of his voice when it was talking about Proust that he always ate before going out to dinner, so that eating would not get in the way of his words. Indeed, the stories of the childlike vanity of artists would fill a five-foot shelf.

But it is not all childlikeness and vanity. Of other things in the artist I'd like to try to suggest one that has had, so far as I know, little or nothing written about it. I'll speak only of the writer, though I think it is much the same with all artists; and I'll keep in mind Philip O'Connor's child-cry, "How can I explain the awful and embarrassing sense of weight — as of rising up through a sea of porridge — that the discussion of literary matters induces in me?"

Recently there was a play by Jack Gelbers that the *New York Times* critic called a farrago of dirt. The play presents a roomful of junkies waiting for a fix. A year or so earlier there had appeared a novel called *The Devil's Advocate,* an advance copy of which the publisher sent to me with a breathless note: "Almost never have we had a book that excited us as much as this one! Can you say something nice about it?" I said I thought it would be a best-seller, and that was what would please them most. The novel portrays a group of devout Catholics and one poor lonely free-thinker, who before the book's end goes out and kills himself.

Suppose you had had an assignment to write both the play and the novel. The novel you would not have found difficult; it portrays cardboard people who say the words and do the things that Christians are believed by some to say and do. The man who kills himself isn't even a cardboard figure; he is merely a foil, a thing of evil on his way to hell, against whose black color the others shine for simple people in heavenly blue. In the novel you have to get inside nobody, explore no depths, offend no persons except the few who use their minds—and it will gross you at least a million. In the play you have a tougher job. If you're an honest writer, you'll realize that the important thing is not whether you outrage the medieval scruples of an emotional illiterate on the *Times*, but whether as creator you have the talent to put yourself aside and enter the personality of a misbegotten whose drug habit has lost him to himself and the world. If you have that kind of talent, the play won't make you rich and an idol of women's clubs but it may put you in the company of those who have gone deep enough to find a piece of truth.

The truth is what any artist is after, but most people, Bertrand Russell has said, are far more interested in being right. It may be right for the believer to be healthy and happy and dull, and for the unbeliever to be a miserable wretch who hangs himself. But it isn't the truth. The loss in a drug addict of self-respect and health and hope is truth, but it isn't right. In all the years of recorded history, right and truth have been implacable enemies, and the seeker of truth has usually been a social outcast. It has been said in ten thousand books that Jesus sought the truth and was hanged.

It is best for me to be personal, and no more modest than a bare minimum of good taste demands. I have published about twenty-five novels and written at least ten others, eight of which have been thrown away. This means I have given names to hundreds of book-people. It means that I have portrayed them at various depths. Many of them are hardly more than names, but to a few of them I gave all the insights I had. If an author writes chiefly about death and killing, and always in the first person, and if his protagonist and the principal woman in each novel are much the same from book to book, under new names, he may be as influential and as acclaimed as any author of our time and he may be read a thousand years from now, but nobody can seriously say that he went deep under the surface. If an author writes of what is called romantic love, which is little more than sex and illusions, he may publish thirty or forty novels, as some have, and use the same set of cardboard characters from book to book. If an author writes what is called historical fiction, that in fact is historical only in such matters as dress, houses, and transportation, and portrays people who think and feel and talk like those of his own time, he may be read by the millions but his novels are not historical novels at all.

Let me try to make it plain. A person may write a novel about King Solomon and portray him as a very wise man, and a great prince of wit and learning in a brilliant kingdom, with a magnificent temple, and the admiration of that enlightened people, the Egyptians; and reviewers in high places may praise his book in their favorite superlatives and it may be a best-seller and Hollywood may buy it for a million dollars and spend twenty millions making an elaborate spectacle of it; and millions of people may read the book and see the picture and hugely enjoy both—but it isn't Solomon and it isn't his time. It may be right, but it isn't the truth.

Suppose another writer undertakes a novel about Solomon.. He reads the greatest authorities in all the related fields—he reads in the Higher Criticism, in geography, flora, fauna, geology, beverages, clothes, music, customs, languages, superstitions, origins. He learns that the Hebrews and their land three thousand years ago were not at all what uninformed people today think they were—that the Hebrews were so unimportant that they were unknown to nearly all the peoples around them; that compared to the great temples of that time the temple Solomon had built was a shabby little edifice, probably of mud-bricks; and that far from being the world's wisest man and most brilliant ruler he very possibly could neither read nor write, and was really only a desert shiek whose people had recently come in from the terrible desert.

If a novelist is going to portray that time as it was, he will have to put aside practically all his views, beliefs, values, and nearly all his knowledge. He will have to strip off, as it were—strip down and go back, culturally naked, to a primitive time of life—to the life of Arab nomads who had a short time before come in from the wilderness to take by murder and force the cultivated lands of a more civilized people; who had come in from the awful sun, winds, sand storms, erosion, foul water holes, heat, starvation, loneliness—this writer, if he is to be serious and an artist, will have to try to get inside the minds, souls, habits, superstitions, fears, and ignorance of this people; and then, further, inside the minds and souls of a few of them, as individuals, apart and unique.

Consider for a moment the job of getting inside Solomon. He and his people had no concept of the adolescent foolishness that Americans call romantic love (the Arab people still have none); no concept of adultery as you know it; no concept of murder and cruelty as you know them. Solomon had never heard of mercy to an enemy. Compassion was unknown to him. The Hebrews before they mixed with other peoples were Arabs, and like all the goat-eating drinkers of camel-milk they were a ferocious, warlike, merciless people, who had a savage desert deity and no divine mother. The novelist who is artist has to get inside all that, and inside that man; to leave the world he has known for another world; to live for a year or two years thinking and feeling with a set of values and a way of life that are alien to him. He is a historical novelist only as measured by the depth and completeness with which he leaves his world and enters this other world. All the rest is tinsel and trappings and Hollywood.

Suppose the novelist goes farther back—back to the ape-people, as I have tried to do—to get inside, if he can, the dim mind and shuttered soul of our ancestor at a time when he had much shorter legs than ours, much longer arms, coarse hair all over him, the prognathous jaw of a Mussolini; when he walked stooped, long arms hanging, a club in one hand; when he hadn't learned to walk completely upright, and so didn't yet have lumbago, appendicitis, and hemorrhoids; when he was learning to utter a few word-sounds; and when, above all, the freeing of his front feet to become hands was setting his brain free to grow. That, scientists tell us, was the greatest thing that has happened in the long way up from darkness and a posture on all fours.

It puts stresses and strains on the writer who forces himself to reach as deep as his insights go. It may be more of an erosion of his mind and spirit when he works in a remote time, for the reason that back there nothing is familiar to him and the terrible strange face of it he takes with him to his dreams. For the serious writer working in his own time, the erosions of mind, soul, and sanity are severe enough—too severe for many, as the statistics on alcohol, insanity, and suicide declare to us. Let me see if I can suggest to you how it is here.

Trying to portray a complex human being was pretty simple until recently, for the reason that it was not known that he was complex. The illuminations of the social sciences have made it depressingly clear that people are not what people used to think they were. The characters in novels two hundred years ago—or even a hundred years ago— are pretty transparent angels and villains compared to some of the murky ambivalent specimens that writers are pushing into their prose today. And think of what is to come! The word *type* is not a good word to apply to people, for the reason that every person is unique; but we still have to use it and a lot of other words just as inexact. We have to think and speak in types—indeed, such words as schizoid, psychopath, paranoiac are now a part of the common language. Such types are the extremes of imperfect personality integration. Now if a novelist is himself of the schizoid type, as some have been and some are today, he should be able to portray that type more convincingly than any other. Or a paranoiac, if he is that; and so on. But a novelist, if he is to have scope, if he is to try to run the whole spectrum, cannot be confined within one type, though the Brontes were almost caught there. It is when he departs farthest from what he basically is that the greatest demands are made on his intuitive insights, and that he risks the greatest danger to his sanity.

Except for the ignorant and dull, who invariably prefer their own kind, the most interesting people are not the sanest. With exceptions they are not the most adult. Let's look at a few instances. The psychopath, the outstanding type of the 20th century, is antisocial, egocentric, self-indulgent, with neither conscience nor moral values. For him what he wants is right. It appears that most confidence men, swindlers, extortionists, and big gangsters, in politics and out, are psychopaths. That Mussolini, Hitler, and Stalin were needs hardly be said. It's an easy type to portray, if you know some well; and who does not? You need only to report their mannerisms, speech, their sly cold ways, for they are a superficial people who live on the surface. Of those I have portrayed, Forenoon in my tetralogy seems to have aroused the most interest — and in such as William Rose Benet the most loathing. Forenoon's major interests were theft and seduction.

The schizoid type is emotionally immature, shy, withdrawn from life, often self-indulgent and narcissistic, physically inelastic, and unable to give easy vent to emotions. Among writers, Emily Dickinson is a classic type. The schizoid can literally explode into violence; or it may live bottled up in its fantasies clear to the end. The only schizoid I ever gave a full book to is June Weeg in my novel called *April* and she was not extreme enough to have become an institutional case; but I have drawn a number of schizoids, having a lot of this type in me — in novels seven, eight, nine, ten, and twelve of my Testament series, and in a few other books. Possibly you can imagine what a wrenching of personality it is to enter the schizoid temperament for a year or two, closing all the doors, as it were, and looking at the world and its people from the timid childlike psyche of this type. Is it strange that an author living a schizoid life should blow up now and then in an alcoholic binge, to shatter the tensions and the loneliness? Or that well-integrated hopelessly sane people with no understanding of such behavior should condemn it?

Involutional melancholia is thought to be the result of persistent efforts to push down and away or at least to rebuke and restrain a strong urge to achievement, and to fulfillment of emotional hungers. It is *the* frustration psychosis. The paranoid type you see everywhere — the outgoing, the aggressive pusher, over-emoting, forever talking about himself or wishing to; who in extreme cases develops irrational suspicions, or hallucinations and delusions in regard to his powers and importance. This type is common in political life. The self-martyred mothers belong here. The hysteric, another type, is over-suggestible, over-submissive, over-devoted, and is likely to have its mind and will dominated by stronger types. There are variants of these and all these can take on in some measure the nature of one another.

We now come to the heart of the matter. Two things at least should be understood about the dedicated novelist. One is that he must live not in his own being but in the beings of others; not in his own personality — indeed, if he starts to write in childhood, he doesn't stand much chance to develop a personality. All the serious writers I have known or read about were unhappy children. They were not allowed to develop well-integrated personalities, and if they had developed them they would never have been writers. They grew up as a weird species of creature who through a process of emotional osmosis became chameleons to those they lived around. If a son, he probably identified with mother or sister; if a daughter, with father or brother. In identification the child so admires and covets and emulates the habits and values of the parent that the son may become almost as much woman as man, the daughter almost as much man as woman. Whether the story is fact or legend it does define the matter for us: Edna Ferber (it says), a masculine-looking woman, said to Michael Arlen, an effeminate-looking man, "My grief, you look a little like a woman!" and Arlen retorted, "So do you, Miss Ferber — a little." That artists partake of the emotions, sensibilities, and attitudes of both sexes in far more than normal measure is made plain by the lives of all the artists known to us. Some of the women — George Sand, George Eliot, Virginia Woolf, or make your own list — have been almost more male than female; and some of the men — Shelley, Chopin, Swinburne, and many others — have been almost more female than male.

So that is one thing. The second thing is that the dedicated writer is not a mere reporter or journalist, content to say only that the woman suddenly showed a tic, that is, a muscular spasm, in one of her eyes when the subject turned to sex; or that the man suddenly closed his eyes tight, opened them, closed them again, and at last stared at the speaker when asked whether, if caught in a jam, he would try to bribe the policeman. Such matters can easily be reported and for most readers mere reporting is enough.

But for the writer whose interest is in motivations as well as mannerisms, reporting is not enough. In his thoughts, reading, dreams, and above all in the searching of himself, he must learn how to project himself into that woman, that man, to discover out of what childhood situations the tic and the closing of the eyes developed as personality mannerisms expressing alarm and warnings from the subconscious mind. A lifetime of that is more than enough to wear a writer out. It is more than enough to erode the feeble personality he had to begin with, and to make him eventually, as acting must make the great actor, a bundle of personality fragments — a compost of human peat and straw and leafmold — a mongrel with a thousand strains. That's about all that will be left of the torments of his long or short life, after art and alcohol and insanity are done with him. There is an actor named Peter Sellers who is anybody but Peter Sellers. He says, "I have no desire to play Peter Sellers. I don't know who Peter Sellers is, except that he's the one who gets paid. Cary Grant is Cary Grant — that's his stock in trade. . . . Write any character you have in mind and I'll shape myself to what you have written. But don't write a part for me." He has said that he has so many inhibitions that he wonders if he exists at all. Inhibitions was an unfortunate choice: what Mr. Sellers meant is that as an actor he has projected himself into so many different personalities that Peter Sellers has been largely assimilated and lost.

The sight of the pathetic remnants of artists in their last years makes the happy well-integrated people shudder and ask questions. There was Sinclair Lewis. Why did he have to end up alone and lonely with a caretaker in Italy, while he drank himself to death? He made piles of money, didn't he? He traveled everywhere, he got the big awards, he had a full life. Those who ask such questions about Lewis should have to spend a few years inside Kennicotts, Babbitts, Arrowsmiths, Gantrys — though these were certainly not such hostile personality-houses as a thousand others in which writers have lived. Who, if sentenced to such a prison, would hesitate in choosing between a Lewis and Dostoievski protagonist? — between a Gantry or Arrowsmith and (if I may say so) Vridar Hunter?

If it is asked — and it often is — why the writer doesn't devote his talent to the psychically-integrated persons who seduce their secretaries and play golf, the reply is that these are not the kind of people out of whom most of the great art has been made. They are the kind of people for whom it is an ordeal to read a book. You have read Thurber on his years with Ross and you haven't forgotten his story of the man who lived uptown in Manhattan, who one day was seen coming out of a residence building far downtown. Said his friend, "What in the world are you doing away down here?" Said the man gloomily, "I'm finishing a book." "A book?" said his friend, astonished. "I didn't know you wrote books." Said the other, still more gloomily, "I don't. I'm reading one."

The reading of most of the greater books, and surely of most of the greater novels, is, for the one who really gets inside them, an experience not unlike that of the one who wrote them. In one respect it is an experience in erosion. It is erosion of superstitions, prepossessions, self-protective assumptions, wishful thinking, self-glorification — for the reader. For the writer it is erosion of a psyche that at best was a loosely-integrated jumble of emotional odds and ends taken from an unhappy childhood — until at last, of the child that never became an adult emotionally (no artist ever has) there isn't much left — not much of Peter Sellers left — only the shadows of all the characters he entered and put forth, or that the writer entered and drew. A truly great actor who has spent most of his life inside Shakespeare's principal males and females isn't likely, after his day is done, to be more than a phantom; or a great creative writer who has spent his years inside the Raskolnikovs and Judes and Egoists. In trying to reach to sources and motivations and to create a human landscape with many personalities and minds, he has quite literally lost his own; and if at last the pathetic little left of him is not absorbed by alcohol, claimed by insanity, or effaced by suicide, he probably will fade away much faster than old generals.

And it seems unlikely that for a long time yet he will be understood by any but the kindred spirits who suffer with him.

The Novelist and His Work

The daily chore — or the trade, as Ernest Hemingway puts it — of turning out books for a living is not, I am sorry to say, the most inspired way of life a human being can undertake. These remarks concerning the profession of novel writing may be considered the "confession" of a writer who has been publishing books regularly since 1927, but let me warn the reader from the beginning that I have nothing dramatic to tell. I am, as the reader will perceive, a fairly methodical person. My wife swears that I am temperamental — by which she means, I suppose, that the Irish in me sometimes overpowers the stolid Dutch-German-English and generates an emotional storm, a temporary violent upheaval, that engulfs the boredom, scatters the tormenting and unintegrated tag ends of thought and feeling, and tries to bring effort into focus and perspective. It would do me no good to deny that this is so, for I have friends scattered over the country who have seen the ape in me rise to the surface and show his simian features. But by and large my attitude toward my craft

---

* First published in *Tomorrow*, December, 1949, under the editor's title, Novel Writing Is My Trade.

has long been that which Jacques Barzun has recently set down, and to which we shall come in a moment.

I may as well, then, be candid. If I were not, there are persons who would quickly detect the pose, the pretensions and pedantry, the mannerisms and conceits. If it takes a thief to catch a thief, it certainly takes an artist even more than a professional psychologist to detect what is theatrical, artificial and mannered in the artist. The posers may fool their votaries but they never fool their colleagues. We who write can not only see what is padding and what is flesh; we separate at once the affected from the real.

And if that is true it is strange, then, that in artists more than in any other group pose does flourish luxuriantly. The old myths, or new ones, prevail, and are fertilized and nourished. That was to have been expected before the great psychologists came to look sharply at human motives and call them by their right name. We are not astonished when we find George Eliot saying that another person, a "not herself," wrote her books, that she was "merely the instrument through which the spirit acted"; or to find Goethe saying that he was convulsed by "psychic pain"; or Mrs. Harriet Beecher Stowe declaring that she did not know that Uncle Tom was dead until she read about it. Such illusions and fantasies are products of the child-mind in its gropings toward personal apotheosis.

Many years ago, when I lived in Greenwich Village, I sometimes went to the wine haunts to observe the attitudinizings of third- or fourth-rate *littérateurs* struggling with their "genius" — sucking exotic tea through long reeds, sipping absinthe from a fragment of a human skull, bowed in clouds of incense before the Muse, or wooing "inspiration" with still more absurd poses. Such goings-on do not astonish us now. We expect those with small talent to compensate with such posturing, conjuring, and necromancing as they can contrive. They are the gods of small cults and they all vanish from the scene soon enough.

But one is now and then fetched up by pure and unabashed myth-making which appears in the popular journals. I have in mind Alva Johnston's profile of Rex Stout in the *New Yorker*, or, and even more, Malcolm Cowley's rather worshipful account of Hemingway in *Life* a year or so ago. We are solemnly told — if Cowley had his tongue in his cheek I missed it — that Hemingway does some quite incredible things. I don't necessarily mean his falling in love "like a big hemlock crashing down through the underbrush" — though that did give me a start. I have in mind such statements as these, that before commencing to write in the morning Hemingway reads what he has already written, "the whole novel, until he is halfway through writing it, or two or three chapters in any case"; and that upon resting from his creative labors he actually counts the words, one by one, which he has written that morning. We may — though I cannot — suppose that Hemingway is that childlike after having lived half a century; or we may suppose — as I do — that he was pulling Cowley's leg. Whatever the truth, myth-making, by the artist himself or by his overzealous cultists and commentators, and pose and posturing and various grotesque dressings-up of the ape, are still with us.

It has often been said that the artist stands above the morality and customs of his time and makes his own rules. The great French painter Delacroix declared: "There are no rules for great souls: rules are only for people who have merely the talent that can be acquired." But I like best the distinctions of Otto Rank. There are three levels of humanity, he says. The lowest are those with the mass mind who accept as reality the customs, traditions and laws of their time and shape their lives in accordance with them. The second level is the neurotics; they can neither accept nor reject themselves, nor contemporary customs and traditions, but strive to find a deeper and more valid reality within themselves. If they succeed in doing this they elevate themselves to the third level and, breaking out of ther neurosis, win through to willing and affirming, becoming thereupon their own moral law. These, says Rank, are the great artists. By his definition the posers and myth-makers are those who, though endowed with talent, are unable to understand, integrate and manage their neurosis. The whole matter, then, comes down, in a very simple way, to self-discipline.

In *The Writer's Book* (Harper's, 1950) prepared by members of the Authors Guild, Jacques Barzun has written a lucid and sometimes luminous essay on this subject. He begins by telling us that all writers now and then get stuck, by which he means that they suffer what psychologists call a "block." His essay is an inquiry into the reasons for this, with some hints on what can be done about it. And his hints really add up to less, much less, self-indulgence, and more, much more, self-discipline. If a writer suffers a "block" it is "to be judged and treated with an even sharper eye for evasion and fraud on the part of the writing self." That is true, obviously. Writers are children. They are emotionally immature, self-idolatrous, evasive, and too often petulant and whining. Barzun concludes his essay with a statement which every Theodore Dreiser, wringing his handkerchief over an unflattering review, or every Thomas Wolfe, weeping with rage for the same reason, ought to hang above his writing desk: "So-called established writers who after years of work still wince at criticism are certainly not established in their own souls." Rank would say they are still neurotic. They are still the prisoners of that naive, infantile self-love which makes such painful reading in a biography of Marcel Proust.

Now it does not follow when the neurotic has won through to affirmation and become his own moral law that he must also be one without self-doubt. Those of the first order of greatness — like Leonardo da Vinci and Goethe — have made it plain that the well-integrated personality and the well-ordered life are quite beyond the artist's grasp. But if an artist takes his art seriously he cannot afford to confuse self-discipline with license. The self-disciplined artist is one who has searched out his motives, looked frankly at his evasions, and taken control over the innumerable emotional tyrannies that leech his purpose and paralyze his will. Until he does that we can expect to find him uttering a lot of nonsense about inspiration, atmosphere, mood, and the kind of environment necessary to mother his genius. An artist worth his salt will work where he can and when he can.

I think I learned that lesson early. I learned that talent can easily be exhausted, as an American psychologist has put it, "in defensive distortions of self-healing." It can become a frenzied wish to exhibit one's self rather than one's art, as in Thomas Wolfe; and it takes some artists a long time to learn that art is not their neurotic distortions. Some, even with major reputations, seem not to have learned that simple truth.

When I reached manhood, I was a horribly neurotic and distorted person. I should imagine, looking back, that I missed a psychosis only by a hair. Very possibly I could have, with different adult influences, developed a multitude of poses and become the hostage of my own conceits. If I missed that road, which so many have taken, I cannot be quite sure when or how, but I think I know. For one thing there is a lot of the methodical German in me. For another — and I think this had greater power in shaping me — I spent four years of my life in postgraduate work in a great university under great scholars. The going was rough and I hated it but I stuck it out.

I recall a day at the end of the first year when I had a conference with Robert Morss Lovett over my Master's thesis. I made a statement that angered him. I said, "But surely you don't expect to find sound scholarship in a Master's thesis?" His large face turned red and he shook a finger at me, crying: "In this school in graduate work we expect scholarship and nothing but scholarship! Your trouble, Fisher, is that you haven't learned what scholarship is."

I hadn't — not yet; and the learning was arduous. I hadn't learned to respect the integrity of a fact and the privileged position of a probability. I hadn't learned that scholarship was not an accumulation of data but discipline. As an undergraduate I had been an undisciplined, self-indulgent youth nourished by my own morbid tastes and fantasies. I had been the darling of my teachers in advanced composition and their flattery had gone to my head like my first drink of bourbon. I had written, for instance, a one-act play, of which my teacher had said, waving the wretched thing before his colleagues: "If Lord Dunsany had written this his name would be known around the world!" How I wince when I recall that moment. I offered that play to Lovett and his criticism was so withering that I walked over to Lake Michigan to drown myself.

Well, that was the beginning. When Lovett pitched my Master's thesis after my play I was ready to quit. But somehow I didn't. I learned, and I learned the hard way — the way of any self-pitying narcissistic artist, with a headful of nonsense about "genius" and "inspiration." I squared my neurotic shoulders and pitched in; and in the next three years I made practically straight A's and graduated *magna cum laude*. It was a dreadful experience, and when I at last finished my final oral examinations, I was a pale, exhausted, shaken, and wretched creature. I still have, now and then, a nightmarish dream about those four years, and always in the dream I am about to fail my courses and be sent the way of my one-act play. But I found out what discipline means, and I would not give anything for the lesson I learned in the Gothic halls of the University of Chicago Midway, or for the moment, after it was all over, when that great scholar, John Matthews Manly, put an arm across my shoulder and said: "Now that you have learned what scholarship is you should be a better artist." And a year or two before his death, after he had re-tired to California, he wrote me a letter saying that he had read my most recent novel and had liked it, but felt that I had some distance still to go before I learned how close in method and in spirit great art and scholarship are. He was right, and his words were golden.

What are my work methods as a writer? I must repeat that they are very dull and commonplace. When I am working on a book, I never allow anything to intervene, save sickness and acts of God. I stick to an inflexible routine, seven days a week, month after month, until the first draft is completed. I revise anywhere from one to four times. After rising in the morning I take a brisk walk, eat a very light breakfast, and sit at my typewriter from two to four hours. (I learned to type when fourteen, and read my longhand with difficulty.)

There are authors who say that they write eight, ten, fourteen or more hours at a stretch. Thomas Wolfe once told me that he some-times wrote all day and all night. I have always been skeptical of such statements. An author *can* work, if not continuously at least continually, for a period of ten or fifteen hours, with interruptions to relax, to brood, to read. I think that in any case the duration of labor must depend on the physical constitution of the person and on his degree of concentration. I am one who concentrates so intensely that I am unaware, usually, of the things around me, including move-ments and sounds. At the end of three hours I am exhausted. It is physically impossible for me to concentrate at such depth for a longer period.

I believe that the artist in any field draws chiefly from his sub-conscious mind. This must be so, since that mind is the storehouse of all that we are. The conscious mind is only the superficial atmosphere, so to speak, which emanates from that deeper and vastly richer mind under the level of awareness.

After I have completed my daily stint, I do not count the words; I would be curious about the state of my emotional health. I would suspect that I was astonished that I was able to beget anything at all — like a hen rising from the nest to look at her egg. I walk to our rural mailbox and then look over the mail while waiting for lunch. After eating I go outside for three or four hours of heavy labor — and I do mean heavy labor. We live in the Idaho country. Ten years ago we bought a few acres of wasteland, chiefly a piece of mountainside, waterfalls, a small lake, and about four acres of land which the owner had abandoned as worthless.

Our ten* years here have been ten years of hard labor. We have built our own house, such as it is, including the masonry, wiring and plumbing; erected five other buildings; and planted several thousand trees, including pine, spruce, juniper, and other evergreens. I have constructed a dam and screens around one side of the lake and have it stocked with rainbow trout. I have built concrete walks and headgates and walls; dug ditches and made fences; laid a lot of pipeline to irrigate our trees; and in various other ways have been a son of toil — so much so indeed that some of the good folk of the valley have long been distressed by my ordinary appearance. They think that a writer should look the part.

Being a person of low pulse rate, low metabolism, and low blood pressure, I have found heavy labor good for me. I have little talent for building, but I have enjoyed it immensely. I agree with a recent statement by Frederick Manfred that a "nonmental" avocation is good for a writer. His preference is a turkey farm or an orchard. I have an orchard and my preference is animals and trees. Readers of my Vridar Hunter tetralogy may be interested — and amused — to learn that I have reproduced here a good part of the environment which Vridar knew as a child.

After the hard outside labor is done — during which much of the time I am thinking about the book I am writing at the moment — I come in, take a shower, eat a very light supper; and, if no friends

---

* Twenty-three now, with long periods spent abroad or at the libraries.

have dropped in, read until I fall asleep. Our friends are nearly all drinking people and when they drop in we, and they, usually drink too much. My reading, since I have for twenty years prepared a series of historical novels, is "heavy stuff" — the books by the ablest scholars in the fields I am covering. In the past ten years I have read such volumes by the hundreds.*

It was Bernard DeVoto, I think, who once wondered aloud in print how I find intellectual nourishment in an out-of-the-way place like rural Idaho — without theatres, museums, libraries, and without friends, for the most part, with intellectual interests. I bring that nourishment to my home. Librarians all over the nation have been unfailingly kind and send to my door any book they have that I ask for. If they do not have the book — and the Library of Congress, surprisingly enough, does not have many books that I need — they tell me where I can find it.

I know authors whose reading is confined almost entirely to the works of their colleagues. My evenings are spent, not with novels or newspapers or journals, but with the fine meaty tomes that have come from some of the ablest minds that have lived. Reading Henry Osborn Taylor's *The Medieval Mind,* or Buchanan Gray's *Sacrifice in the Old Testament,* or the books by G. G. Coulton, H. C. Lea or Adolf Harnack, Montefiore or Rostovtzeff — to name only a few — is, for me anyway, an adventure. I find more pleasure in Kohler's *History of Costume,* Tennant's *Doctrine of the Fall and Original Sin,* or Goodenough's *The Mystic Gospel of Hellenistic Judaism* than I could find in seeing *South Pacific;* more "inspiration" in Leuba than in any novelist I have ever read: more intellectual excitement in Hall's *Jesus in the Light of Psychology* or Dill's *Roman Society* or Jane Harrison's *Prolegomena* than I could find in all the clubs of New York; more spiritual nourishment in Huntington's *Civilization and Climate* or Michelet's *Satanism and Witchcraft* or Thorndike's *History of Magic* than I ever found inside a church; and more sheer joy in Tyler, Shotwell, Petrie, or Loisy than I ever find save with a few enlightened friends and a bottle of old bourbon.

---

* More than 2,000 before the research was completed.

And there is my joy — my "inspiration," if you will — not only in plants but in birds and beasts. This essay was interrupted at the fifth paragraph above while I went to look at my beaver traps, because this incorrigible nuisance persists in destroying my trees. On my way to the traps I came to a mother Chinese pheasant and her ten-day-old babies, and a more adorable thing than a baby pheasant I have never seen. I lay in the tule and watched them for a while, and the mother sat off at a safe distance and watched me. A cat will probably eat all the young within a week. My wife and I wondered what to do about them and thought of giving the mother and her children a safe home in our hen yard; but we knew that all around us were scores of other pheasants and birds of many kinds, whose defenseless young will be eaten soon; and remembering then that our religious friends believe that all this is a part of God's omniscient and compassionate scheme, we left them to their fate.

We have around us throughout the year many species of duck and bird that are a delight to study; otter and beaver and muskrat, weasel and raccoon, heron and grebe and marsh birds; and we have our own domestic beasts. I pity those persons — and among them is a literary critic who rebuked me — who cannot perceive, or, better, *feel* the affinity between beasts and men. The ancients knew better than that. They accepted all life in common fellowship. That deep and abiding truth becomes clear to anyone who studies his animal cousins and learns, as he must learn with study, to love them. He can learn more about human motives in a barnyard than in a night club.

Robert Penn Warren has written that William Faulkner's idiot Snopes, with his "fixation" on a cow, "shows a human being as close as possible to the 'natural level,' " that the "idiot is human and not animal, for only human desires, not animal, clothe themselves with poetry." That fantastic statement is for me a striking instance of human presumption and self-love. No human *idiot* (the mental age is under four) ever felt half as much poetry as the mourning dove now making its sad and lonely music in our honey locust; or the male pheasant who, last winter when the snow was deep, flew up into our locust trees to shake loose the seed pods for the hens waiting below; or the lovely swallows who at this moment are building a nest under our roof, and flying into the kitchen now and then to look things over or perch on the window and turn first one inquiring eye and then the other on our goldfish.

Inspiration is a word I eschew; like soul and ghost and genius and many other words from our primitive past it has for me no meaning. But if it is insisted — as strangers who come here do insist — that I draw inspiration from *something*, then let it be from these simple and lovely things. From these, and from the books before me by great men and women who devoted their lives to the clean pure pursuit of truth. If, when writing, I get that "block" which Barzun spoke of, I do not turn to a novel or a book of poems. I take down a volume by a great scholar and read.

It might be Professor Finkelstein's account of the Pharisees, or Hatch's brilliant Hibbert lectures. Whatever the book may be, I read a few of the passages which I have marked, and have read again and again. It might be O. Müller's "If one who invents the myth is only obeying the impulse which acts also upon the minds of his hearers, he is but the mouth through which all speak." It might be Professor Guignebert's "We must not confound the Nazarene with the ideal which he has come to represent since the birth of Christian dogma, an ideal for which he was not responsible." It might be Professor Taylor's "All men, except fools, have their irrational side. Who does not believe what his reason shall labor in vain to justify?" It might be Cardinal Newman saying that the early Church Fathers "thought that, when there was a *justa causa*, an untruth need not be a lie." And then Jerome on St. Paul: "The proofs which you have used against the Jews and against other heretics bear a different meaning in their own contexts to that which they bear in your Epistles. We see passages taken captive by your pen and pressed into service to win you a victory, which in volumes from which they are taken have no controversial bearing at all." After a few minutes with the great minds that toiled in obscurity to give us the precious truths we have inherited, I return to my work strengthened. That is the only inspiration I know that can be summoned when it is needed.

* * *

How do my ideas originate and grow? Out of what are my characters born? And what kind of research do I do? The last I have an-

112

swered. The others I do not believe any novelist can honestly answer.

I am, of course, now engaged with historical fiction; and since I am in the historic era my characters, or many of them, are there for me. My next novel to be written — the three preceding it are written but not yet published — is to be about Christian origins; and among the thousands of notecards in my file for this story are those under the heading: *possible characters to use.* Among the names here, all historic, are Bar Kozibah, Polycarp, Basilides, Epicharis, Eliezer ben Hyrcanus, Phineas ben Jair, Pliny, Gamaliel, Epictetus, and many more. My notes include such information as I have been able to gather about their physical appearance, personality, opinions, position, and influence. I shall have to invent a few characters when it is necessary to fill out the frame.

If I were asked where the idea originated for my present series of historical novels I could answer that. After completing my Vridar tetralogy I realized that I had not been able to tell how such a person came to be what he was. I realized that to understand the adult it is necessary to do much more than go back to the child. Childhood, after all, isn't the principal thing that makes Sammy run. The principal thing is the past, out of which the child has come. So, abandoning the superficial notion that a person can be made explicable in terms of his childhood and present, I took up in earnest the reading for this series. If I live to complete the task, the rewritten Vridar story will be the final volume.*

The idea grew after I had plunged into the reading, after, let us say, I had read some two hundred volumes about the ancient past and had compiled a bibliography of several hundred more. The whole magnificent story that will be written as novels by someone, some day — shaped up as I read. There were many questions to be answered. I knew from the beginning that the novel about Jesus would be one of the crucial stories. I also believed that it would be necessary to give at least two volumes to the Old Testament. But about what biblical characters and what time? I had to read scores of books by the Higher Critics before I could come to an answer to that question. The answer settled upon Solomon and his period, and the Maccabees.

* Now published as *Orphans in Gethsemane.*

113

In regard to the latter there can be no doubt. A great scholar has said that the Maccabean struggle was the most important struggle in history for Western civilization. I think that is so. But it is a question whether the other novel should be about Solomon or Hosea or Ezra. A novel about David would be more publishable but David was far less important than Solomon in the history of the Western world. I perceive now — good Lord! — that the task which I have undertaken should be done in thirty or forty novels, not twelve. And some day it may be.

How do I go about writing an historical novel? Again, I cannot quite say. The notes for the novel on the origins of Christianity come almost to two hundred thousand words. There are scores of categories. I shall have to spend hours every day for months going over and over these notes until the story begins to fall within its frame. I think my subconscious mind will have a great deal to do with it. I shall dream about these things; and some solutions will be given forth to consciousness with my knowledge, and some, I am sure, without it. It is much like working one's way into the pile of notes for a Ph.D. thesis. Or it is like moving into a new area where everything is unfamiliar. Five or ten years later you know it well, but you can seldom know when or in what way you became familiar with any part of it.

Somerset Maugham has said that the historical novel is the most difficult to write; I mean the *historical novel,* not fables that pass as such. But it has advantages. One has before him the chronology, many of the characters, many of the events. The principal difficulty lies, for me at least, in the task of integrating such huge masses of material. One writes a contemporary novel without thinking of costume, modes of travel, food, inns, customs, sports, professions; they take care of themselves. One doesn't have to drag in a lot of stuff to give plausibility and verisimilitude. There is also the problem, if one is bent on historical truth and accuracy, of weighing the scholars in controversial matters. And since I have been asked the question, "How do you tell which scholars are the greatest?" I shall conclude with my answer.

One finds out with a good deal of reading and exploring that an individual scholar or a few scholars seem to be accepted by all their colleagues as first-rate. Suppose we take the New Testament field: one turns to the works of B. W. Bacon, late of Yale, or Kirsopp Lake of Harvard; and in reading them one senses which of the scholars quoted they have the most respect for. Name by name one comes to know and to read the principal ones: G. F. Moore, Torrey, Burkitt, Montefiore, and others who belong to the first rank. The matters on which they all agree I accept — how presumptuous I should be not to! — though is it necessary to say that such novelists as Lloyd Douglas and Sholem Asch do not accept their findings at all? If essential matters are still in dispute — whether Nero burned the Christians, whether Jesus of Nazareth was a historic figure — I must then choose what seems to me, on the basis of the evidence presented, the more probable. In the interest of drama or arrangement the great temptation is sometimes to choose the less probable!

But those years of postgraduate training always look down from my shelves, and there come to me again the last words of Mr. Manly, that the discipline and the love of truth are the same in both scholarship and art.

Hometown Revisited

Some twenty years ago a review of one of my novels appeared in a well-known journal under the heading, The Man from the Antelope Hills. At that time it was the common opinion of reviewers that I might develop into an American Thomas Hardy; it was said that the Antelope hills in eastern Idaho were my Wessex. But I was not another Hardy and the hills were never a Wessex for me.

One of the annoying things about some reviewers is their desire to classify and trademark every new novelist who comes along. Thereafter they expect him to be faithful to his trademark, and if he is not, they are likely to feel resentful; to argue with him; to try to prevail on him to write what they think he should write. I published a novel laid in that hill country, a second, a third, never dreaming that certain reviewers would be filing me away under "Hardy" or "Wessex." When I cast off the label — perversely, I have no doubt they felt — they destroyed their old file and thereupon set me up under "Dreiser." Still later they had to throw that card away, and at last gave me up as a bad egg — foolhardy, unpredictable, and completely off the track. Today some of them refuse to review me

---

* First published in *Tomorrow*, Dec., 1949.

at all. In can't say that I blame them. The task of reviewers would be enormously simplified if authors would only stick to their early trademark.

I could, I suppose, have written twenty novels about the Antelope people. At one time I seriously considered trying to do exactly that. That was in the years when it was assumed that I was busy mapping my Wessex, and digging out all the stuff on the Judes and Tesses who lived there. The reviewers never understood that I detested the Antelope country and was trying to come to some kind of terms with it, so that I could proceed to a more sunlit area. And besides, this country, unlike Wessex, was not content to remain fixed in its old meanings. It is not what it was when I wrote of the toilers on the hills, or of old Charley Bridwell who beat the living daylights out of his sons and threw them into the river, or of Vridar Hunter, driven into lunacy. I drove up the other day to have a good look at it and talk to some of the old-timers, though few of them are still there. Not many areas in the country, I am sure, have suffered a transformation so astonishingly complete.

* * *

It was a cloudless day in the spring of 1901 when my father piled on to a rickety old wagon (these wagons were called lumber wagons by the frontiersmen I knew) everything he had on earth, including a wife and three children, and fled from civilization — or as much of it as had invaded the thinly settled valleys of eastern Idaho. He was heading for the last frontier, thirty miles from a railroad or a village, and, except the Wheaton family across the river, eight or ten miles from the nearest neighbors, with no roads between. Introverted, reticent, lonely, he preferred the untamed and the unexplored. He had a proud English-Dutch wife who hated backwoods uncouthness and loneliness, as much as he hated the settled life where the neighbors had crowded in. Why she went with him, I'll never know, unless it was to get away from the foul tongue and the Irish tyrannies of her mother-in-law.

They had an infant daughter and two small sons, my brother and me, both extremely neurotic, even at that early age, and much too frightened to ask questions. All day long two scrawny horses dragged that rickety and squealing wagon, with its burden of people and junk. A fancy wagon in those days had a seat on springs. This wagon had none. We sat in its bed, which rested on the axles, absorbing every bounce and jolt, mile after mile. At dusk we camped somewhere by water, ate a little bread and milk, and rose at daylight to journey again. This morning we entered the rolling hills, called Antelope hills, because herds of antelope once grazed there; but on them this day, almost half a century ago, there was only sagebrush, dust, wind, coyotes, badgers, and hawks.

After a few miles we came to a precipice above the South Fork of Snake River, and for three miles we followed a path along that precipice, several hundred feet above the river. In those years it was a fearful stream in the whole mountain-length of it. Fed by the deep snows as far away as Yellowstone Park, and draining the whole area of Jackson Hole and the eastern flanks of the Tetons, it came plunging and roaring down its deep canyons, falling in some stretches fifteen or twenty feet to the mile. I'll never forget my first terrified view of it this morning.

After about three miles we left its precipice and took a faint path across the sagebrush hills. The world of people was now far behind us. I remember sitting in that wagon, with my guts almost jolted out of me, and looking back at the far blue distance out of which we had come. I remember only one remark by my father in that two-day journey. It was in the afternoon of the second day when he spit out his quid, looked at the great mountains looming before us, and said, "It ain't much furder now."

We returned from the hills to the river's gorge, and on its brink looked down. The river's muddy torrents were plunging along the mountain-base, hundreds of feet below us. Above the river, across from us, were the Big Hole mountains, their highest summits rising two thousand feet from the river's bed. All around us now was a wilderness of aspen, fir, chokecherry, serviceberry, and sage. Our father cut an aspen tree and, chaining it to the wagon behind, dragged it, using it as a brake. Our mother and three children got down from the wagon, and our father drove it down the mountain, the four of us following the aspen. Down he went, down a dim trail so precipitous that most of the time the wagon threatened to plunge ahead in spite of the tree it was dragging, and over the beasts. Mother

walked, carrying the babe, her two silent and horrified sons trudg-
ing at her side; and down we went, down and down, smelling the
wild life around us and the river waters and the tangled jungles of
almost impenetrable thicket — down into what seemed to my terrified soul to be the bottom of the world. That awful descent, I was
told later, was a mile and a half in length.

When at last we were down, out of the sky and the mountains,
we found ourselves on a river bottomland, with marshes and bogs
smelling of sulphur, with a mountainside of jungle looming above
us, with the furious river before us, with all the wild things everywhere — beaver, otter, mink, muskrat; deer and elk and bear; badger
and coyote and wolf and mountain lion — and more birds than I have
ever seen anywhere since that day. We stood on a small clearing that
covered about three or four acres, at one edge of which was a crumbling cottonwood-log shack, with an earth roof and an earth floor,
and door hinges made of old shoes. That was our new home, and
was to be our home for more than ten years. There was no stable,
no shed, no outbuildings, not even a privy. That shack, through the
roof of which the waters would pour when it rained, with hunks of
mud dropping to our faces as we tried to sleep, under bedding that
was chiefly untanned elk and deer skins — that shack and the four
acres cleared in a jungle my father had given a cow for. This was
our new home.

On the whole of the Antelope hills which we had crossed in our
journey there was not a shack or a person anywhere — nothing but
rolling prairie with its wild things. That was on the south and south-
west. Before us in the north, across the river, stood the mountains.
The boundary of this river bottom, which was to be our home, was
the river itself on the east, north and west. On another river bottom,
straight across from us, lived the Wheatons — drunken, lazy, philo-
sophic, prank-playing Charley, with his lovely scared-to-death wife,
and his children, two of whom, the oldest sons, were the wildest and
most reckless daredevils I have ever known. But with neither bridge
nor boat — in those early years when Charley visited us, to borrow
food that he never paid back, he swam the river, and returned *swim-
ming on his back,* with the food, such as it was, riding on his chest

— with neither bridge nor boat, that family might as well have been on the other side of the world.

The day we arrived, no word was spoken, so far as I can remember now. The junk was carried into the shack, whose odor of mice and rats was overpowering. The beasts were turned out to grass. Then our father gathered wood for a fire, while my brother and I stood together, looking round us at this awful land of roaring sounds and hidden terrors. He was too small to remember that journey. I have always looked back on it as on a nightmare. My early years there were nightmare. People have thought this strange, who have never known the frontiers, or who got their knowledge of it from such romantic tosh as that in Willa Cather's early books.

For five years (I think it was) I never left that sunken home, being schooled by my mother. After a while our father managed to pick up a cow. Because he was a hunter who in that area had few peers, and loved hunting as he loved nothing else, we lived chiefly on wild flesh and such wild fruits as our mother could find. Our playthings were nothing but the sticks and stones, and the bones of things dead long ago, that we found there. Our sweets were wild honey. Our clothes were simple shabby things that our mother made from our father's castoff garments, or from skins. How I have blessed whatever gods there be that our pious Mormon mother was never able to have more children than the three she took there! If she had had the twelve she wanted, none of us could possibly have escaped from the poverty to school.

What did we eat in those years? Deer (I can taste and smell venison every time I think of the word) and elk; wild chicken, duck, goose, fish; wild fruits, including serviceberry, currant, strawberry, chokecherry, huckleberry; and bread and milk. With our grubbing-hoe our father, a powerful man, waged war on the jungle, clearing the land acre by acre, and planting it to hay and grain. With grubbing-hoe and team he cleared about seventy acres of dense growth, over a period of fifteen or twenty years. After a while he had two cows, then four, then ten; four horses instead of two; an old mowing machine and a hayrake. After a while our mother made cheese, and once a month during open weather made the long journey to the valley in the rickety old wagon, camping at night by the wayside, alone, and peddling cheese from door to door. Of all the blessed sounds in life for me, none has ever been so sweet as the noise of that rumbling wagon on the dugway, long after dark, coming home. Always she brought home a few things, including five sticks of licorice, which her three children, with solemn faces and measurements, divided among themselves. Our sister was such a thrifty little wench that she hoarded her treasure, as we discovered years later. We never forgave her for that.

That was our life in those years, but not all of it, and for the sons not the worst of it. There were times — and even now I can feel my flesh creep, remembering them — when I came face to face with a wolf-bitch and her cubs, and fled on wings; when a mountain lion sat within a few feet of me and screamed its heart out; when bears came lumbering across our grainfields, leaving paths of ruin; when in a black night a turpentined horse (the turpentine was injected into the intestines) sat on its haunches and pawed at the night and screamed (that was the work of the Wheaton boys). Several times I came close to drowning. But worst of all for me, a neurotic and terrified child, was the picture of death everywhere and the blood of death — of shrikes impaling songbirds; spiders sucking the juices from living things; weasels sucking the blood from things still alive; the night-screams of rabbits and other animals caught by their enemies; the patches of blood I found where things had been slain and eaten. . . . And there were the gentle sightless eyes of the deer and elk brought home.

But the frontiers were vanishing; life could not go on that way. Our father had fled civilization, but civilization came to seek him out. In the valleys below, Mormon colonists had homesteaded most of the lands that could be irrigated. Men came pushing in, looking for homes. And one day a man with more imagination than the rest wondered if wheat would grow on the Antelope hills, without artificial watering. He planted a small patch and watched it. Other men experimented, but it took them a long while to learn the mulch system, the harrowing of land to make a covering of dust, to retain the moisture of the melted snows. For years they strove to conquer the hills and failed; but at last, still fighting wind and drought, a few of them secured a foothold, built shacks, and brought their families from the valley to the hills. By the time I was eighteen there was a neighbor only three miles distant, on the south. When I was twenty-one, I homesteaded a hundred and twenty acres of sagebrush, aspen, and serviceberry, and built a small hut on it to stake my claim. By that time all the best land was under squatters' rights.

* * *

Let us jump now to the year 1931 and see what the picture was like. In that year I left Manhattan to return to the homeplace, and spent four years there. I built a modern home for my parents; two barns, a garage, hencoops, sheds — and abandoned the last of the privies which I had erected in former years. Building privies had been my childhood apprenticeship in carpentry. Each year, shamed by my clumsy handiwork, I had built a better privy than the last, until finally I set up a magnificent monster, with an old Ford wind-shield above the door to let in light, and a foolproof lock.

In 1931 I drove up from the valley over a modern highway, for the southern entrance to Jackson Hole and the Teton and Yellowstone parks now goes this way. Five miles from the homeplace I had to leave the highway and take a makeshift road across plowed fields. All around me the land had been conquered, except here and there an aspen cove; and even these were now yielding to the bulldozers. How different it all was in appearance from that day, thirty years before, when we first crossed the wild hills! Half of it was wheat-green, half of it freshly summer-fallowed. This is deep soil. A long time ago Snake River flowed across here and laid down a lot of the finest soil in Wyoming. Dig down six feet or ten and the earth is as rich as that on the surface. Later, when the wheat ripened, the hills lay like great golden half-unrolled carpets.

But as late as 1931 all but a few farmers were using not tractors but horses, not harvesters but binders, not trucks but wagons. Only two or three had got possession of more than 160 or 320 acres. One farmer had almost a thousand acres and was farming not with beasts but with machinery, and making so much money that his neighbors all hated him. Ten years ago he retired with what was estimated to be half a million dollars.

In 1931 this man no longer hauled his water. In all that broad benchland the only stream was, and is, Antelope creek, which goes dry, except in its southern mountain source, early in the season. In all those early years, farmers had to haul their water from the river, or from the creek's source. Because water was so precious, there was not much bathing then. A farmer had to spend a long day with team and wagon-tank to fetch a few hundred gallons, and from this every day he had to water his beasts. Not even on Saturday night did the family always bathe. Many a time I have seen father, mother, and six or eight children wash their hands and faces in the same quart of water in a tin basin. It was an ill-smelling people, unwashed and undusted from weekend to weekend. But this enterprising farmer, who had got hold of so much land, not only farmed entirely with machinery but had sunk a deep well. More than that, he had built a neat five-room cottage and painted it white — and what a picture it made standing on a hilltop, with mean little shacks on the farms around it! Greatest miracle of all, his wife, having well-water on a pump, planted flowers against her house, and two shade trees. Her dooryard was the only one in the whole area with a spot of green in it. Her house was the only one with a bathroom, including an indoor toilet.

That was in 1931.

* * *

Today, behold the miracle! The free enterprise system has worked its wonders, weeding out the unfit, the timid, the stupid, and delivering the hills, farm by farm, into the hands of those with stamina and vision. Most of the farmers who were there in 1931 are gone. Ineffectual and discouraged, they sold out and went to the valleys, to find jobs on WPA, to live in shacks, to "get on relief." Those who bought them out have added year by year to their holdings, until today a few own most of the farms, and seem likely to own all of them. Some farm two thousand acres or more. Land that sold for ten dollars an acre is now a hundred and still climbing.*

All the methods of farming are now modern. There isn't a horse left in the entire country. All spring and summer and early fall the hills hum with the sound of tractors pulling plows, drills, harrows, weeders, and the great combine-harvesters, moving across the broad

---

* The best lands are now $150 an acre or more.

fields of gold. Every farmer has a small fortune invested in machinery, including the trucks with which he hauls his grain to the market.

Take, as an instance, my brother-in-law, though he is nowhere near the biggest farmer there. In 1931 he was trying to eke out a living on forty acres. Today he tills almost a thousand. He has a new cat-tractor that draws four sixteen-inch plows; drills, weeders, trucks, a big new harvester, a new car. He lives in style. He spends far more for luxuries now than he spent for his entire maintenance twenty years ago.

Nobody lives on the hills now after the harvesting is done. They move to the city for the winter. Some of them have handsome homes in Idaho Falls, with tiled bathrooms, solid maple in their dining room, expensive rugs, fancy radios, landscaped yards. A farmer begins work on the hills about mid-April. By mid-November his labor is done and he is a gentleman of leisure, who can lounge in his big overstuffed chairs and read the comics, look at TV, worry about his income tax (like most farmers he probably deducts more than he has coming to him), sit around in the pool halls, and watch the snows on the eastern mountains. Heavy snows mean abundant moisture for the next season.

A few of them don't even live on the hills during the season of labor, but live in the valley, fifteen or thirty miles distant. They drive in their big cars to their farms, ride a tractor fourteen or sixteen hours, and go home for the night. There are practically no hired men. In 1931 there were seasonal laborers, shocking grain behind binders, pitching sheaves into the thresher hopper. But no more. Now as the combine-harvesters winnow the golden grain, its elevators lift it and dump it into open trucks that move along with the machines.

I know a farmer whose wheat check last fall was $100,000. Some of them buy new cars for their sons in Stanford or Berkeley. Some of them buy valley ranches with their profits. It's the same old story when competitive enterprise is given its way: the hard-working, intelligent, and thrifty people get hold of nearly everything, while the less able vote for bigger pensions and Glen Taylor.

* * *

How about my parents, among the first three families to move to that country? Have they prospered? Well, no, except in a very

124

modest way. Father has been a very stubborn and unchanging man, in love with the old (including the Old Testament) and afraid of the new. His last horse is dead but it was the last horse to die in that country. He resisted with scornful mutterings and grumblings every encroachment of gas-driven machinery. He looked on all such things as inventions of the Devil. For years he sulked, as he tinkered with an old wornout threshing machine, or with horses plowed four acres in twelve hours, while with a tractor his neighbor plowed thirty. It was my brother who convinced him that he ought to change his ways.

And then what a transformation in him! He will be eighty his next birthday, his wife seventy-seven; and though they are not what they used to be when they trotted in their labor sixteen or eighteen hours a day, they are together, with the help of one man, farming four hundred acres. They have all modern machinery, including two tractors and a truck. My father almost died making the transition from the frontier to the modern world, but having made it, he is so fascinated by the new, and now so contemptuous of the old, that he is working himself to death.* It is strange that he resisted so, because he identifies easily with machines, and would rather you"d kick him in the belly than kick his tractor. His great regret is that he gave up horses so late. He will net three or four thousand this year, but he looks around him at those who will net fifty and his grief is great.

Until recently my mother rode a tractor on the daylight shift, my father on the night shift. Though devout Mormons, they never allowed Sunday to interfere with the ox in the mire, or felt that any man earned his salt on less than seventy hours a week. When I told my father that John L. Lewis wants a three-day week for his miners, he just looked at me, unable to find words to express his contempt. Those old frontiersmen were a great race. There *were* giants in the earth in those days. But the last of them will soon be gone and though there may be better men there will be none like them.

Father is killing himself with overwork but he won't quit. He has always sworn that he would live to be a hundred, and the other day, rumbling with scorn, he boosted it to a hundred and ten. If

---

* He did, literally, dying at 86.

125

he must die he wants to die while riding a tractor and plowing a furrow. It is the hope of his sons that he will die that way.

As for our mother, she now has a home in Idaho Falls — not such a place as some of the farmers have built, but a little old cottage on Glen Taylor's side of the tracks. Last winter she bought an electric range and refrigerator, the first she has ever owned; and she's as crazy about them as her husband is about his tractors. She doesn't think she will live to be a hundred. She thinks she'll go any day now but she wants to cook a few more meals on that miraculous stove, open again the cool wonder of that refrigerator and take out butter that is not rancid, milk that is not sour. They have fought St. Paul's good fight, they have kept the faith; and they deserve the few comforts that have come to them in their sunset years. Rather than accept a dole or even an old-age pension, they would go back to their river home and draw the shades and die. That spirit in them their children are proud of. That spirit built this nation.

And how is it with me when I return to the country where I suffered terrors in childhood? Do I feel the dread and the horrible loneliness any more? Well, it would be a lie to say that my depths are not stirred. I usually pause at the brink and look over at the mountains; then down at the river and across to the old Wheaton place, where a former son-in-law now lives with a squaw. Every tree that still stands, every bottomless bog and spring, every meadowland jungle that formerly smelled so strong of wild things — they are all there but I try to look at them now with calm. My brother and I don't love the place but we try not to hate it.

Take the river.

During our childhood no reservoirs had been built to impound its waters for irrigation. In the spring runoff, when the millions of acres of deep snow were melting, it came in such furious and headlong roaring past our place that even grown people were afraid of it. My mother lived in fear of it. It drove Mrs. Wheaton almost insane. For it came out of the east, swung at a right angle against a great ledge of stone and boiling back upon itself roared for a half-mile to the north; at the Wheaton place it plunged against another wall of stone, swung again at a right-angle, and poured back into the west; and in half a mile swung again to the south. The roar of it in late springtime shook dishes in cupboards, and was like deep shattering thunder in the mountain walls. Nobody who sees it today can believe what it was like fifty years ago.

Two great reservoirs impound it now. A third is to be built, at the lower end of my childhood home — to put it and the Wheaton place under two hundred feet of water!*

Or take the Douglas fir that stood by the old shack. In the daytime hawks and owls with their cold incredible eyes looked down at me from the branches. After dark, when a wind entered the night, its deep wild breathing stirred my sleep. It was a giant then. Today it is an old tree, pathetic, shrunken, and dying. For us who went away to college and then over a part of the earth, everything here has shrunk, as the things of childhood must for the man. The tree and the river today are symbols of that monstrous and mysterious infinite which the neurotic fancies of two terrified lads saw in everything around them. Man may conquer his environment, but he hasn't yet conquered the ignorance in him which almost destroys his sons.

The frontiers which I knew in the West are no more. I'm glad I knew them, no matter what their terrors for neurotic children; for in having known them, I am better able to understand the world that is being built out of them. A New York poet, who had never known the frontiers, cried out when reviewing one of my books, "If Mr. Fisher thinks life is like that I am here to tell him it isn't!" But it was. It was the kind of life that destroyed the weak, and added the meaning of their death to the strong.

---

* I am glad that my father did not live to see that.

Communism and Emperor Worship

For years now under the ceaseless barrage of propaganda, both American and Russian, a great many people seem to be confused and soul-searching, and to be wondering what the truths and values are, on either side, in this so-called cold war. It is obvious that among the intellectuals there are many who, though neither Communist nor fellow-traveler, do nevertheless maintain a somewhat cynical skepticism: for them, as for the common people, the issues are not clear and the objectives are not plain. This is particularly true of those who are no longer Christian in the strict orthodox sense, yet do perceive that the struggle is not a simple one between godlessness and God. It is depressing that so much energy is spent on abuse, on charge and countercharge, lies and denials, and so little on an effort to reduce the matter to its essentials, so that Americans can under-

---

* This essay was written at the end of the forties, when many political leaders in this country and intellectuals in various fields were still bewitched by Communism. I sent it to *Harper's* and a few other journals, all of which promptly returned it without comment. This revision has changed only a few tenses and omitted a few names of persons then very famous, like Henry A. Wallace, but now unknown to many Americans.

stand the nature of the struggle and what it is that their tax money is being spent for. And it is surprising, to me at least, that nobody, so far as I know, has drawn the deadly parallel between Communism as it exists under the Kremlin, and ancient emperor worship. I should think it pretty futile and fatuous to oppose Communism without understanding it, and I'm not persuaded that our political leaders understand it at all, save in the unsophisticated terms of menace and atheism. This essay is an attempt to point out some of the parallels, and to show that Communism, not so much in its theory as in its actual life and being, is something old in a new dress.

* * *

Professor Shirley Jackson Case has somewhere written of the "astonishing phenomenon known as emperor worship." It is hardly a phenomenon and there is nothing astonishing about it, for it has been with us in various forms a long time. Gibbon reminded us that the most lofty titles "and the most humble postures, which devotion has applied to the Supreme Being, have been prostituted by flattery and fear to creatures of the same nature with ourselves." And it is well to recall, with the Russians in mind, that the adoration of common mortal man has always flourished more luxuriantly in the East and has always been somewhat repugnant to the sensibilities of the West. As Lecky says, the "deified man had long occupied a prominent place in ancient belief, and the founders of cities had been very frequently worshiped by the inhabitants." The Russians have such cities — Leningrad and Stalingrad.

The most primitive form of religion was tribal, that is, essentially nationalistic; and usually there was a god who supervised each national activity. When Rome converted the world into a political unit, the cult of emperor worship was added to and to a large extent superseded the older national religions. Rome's only contribution to religion lay in that. It was a purely political or State religion, as Communism is; but it differed from Communism in this, that whereas emperor worship did not strive to displace local religions or compel the people to accept one unified religious doctrine, these are objectives of the Kremlin's system.

What was emperor worship? Gregg points out that the Roman idea of the State "was that government and religion should be one —

the state an idol before which every citizen should bow, the national religion an institution sharing the sanctity and inviolability of the state." That is exactly the Communist system. Anciently the chief symbol was the statue of the emperor, which was set up in practically all the cities and towns, those occupied by Jews being excepted. Stalin had hundreds of thousands of his photographs throughout the lands he dominated and these took the place of the statue. We may not suppose that intelligent and enlightened people looked upon the emperor as a god, any more than enlightened Communists regarded Stalin as a superhuman being. But there is abundant evidence that the common people did look upon the emperor as a god — indeed, were encouraged to do so, or in any case to identify his attributes with those of divinity. Because every Roman had an attendant "genius," a power that determined his functions and well-being, he believed that when he burned incense before the statue he was promoting the health and power of the emperor's "genius" — which in turn determined the course and prosperity of the empire. The burning of incense, in another manner, was one of Stalin's political tools.

In one of our popular magazines there appeared a photograph of Russian children with faces upturned to the sky. Under the photograph was the editor's caption, "Soviet zone children got demonstration of practical atheism at a Punch-and-Judy show. 'Want some candy?' asked Punch. 'Oh, yes,' the children cried. 'Pray to God for it,' Punch told them. When nothing happened, the children were advised to pray to Stalin. When they did, candy showered down upon them."

That is typical of the childlike American misunderstanding of Communism. Calling this a lesson in atheism brings to mind the fact that the Romans called the Christians atheists. We are dealing here with symbols, no matter whether it is God or man-god Stalin; and though there may be a difference for the theologian or the philosopher, there is none for those offering the prayers. It is not a lesson in atheism at all. Stalin was converting religious emotions to his political advantage, as the Caesars did. Halliday reminds us that politically "the worship of Augustus and Roma, the worship, that is to say, of the great distant emperor and the mighty power of Rome, formed a valuable prop to imperial monarchy and a sentimental link which bound the distant provinces to the crown." The parallel case of Moscow and its satellites is obvious.

Polybius said the Romans used religion — that is, emperor worship — "as a check upon the common people. . . . seeing that every multitude is fickle and full of lawless desires, unreasoning anger and violent passion, the only resource is to keep them in check by mysterious terrors and scenic effects." Another ancient, Diodorus, said that the "myths that are told of affairs in Hades, though pure invention at bottom, contribute to make men pious and upright" — as the stories told of affairs in Hell are supposed to have done. Varro perceived that "It is in the interest of the States to be deceived in religion." Livy said that Numa used "fear of the gods as the most effective thing for an ignorant and rough multitude." But it is the tendency of American political leaders to assume that the common people are enlightened, reasonable, and fully qualified to make a choice between two political systems or two sets of propaganda. This assumption, inherent in a democracy, is one of the thinnest spots in the American political armor, not only at home but also abroad.

Emperor worship was popular with the masses. Walker tells us that this worship "directed to the ruler as the embodiment of the state, or rather to his 'genius' or indwelling spirit, spread rapidly. It soon had an elaborate priesthood under state patronage, divided and organized by provinces, and celebrating not only worship but annual games on a large scale." Elaborate public spectacles are, of course, one way by which Communism tries to maintain its hold on the people — or, as in political conventions, inaugurals, and all that, a democracy, for that matter.

After pointing out that deification of the emperor was as natural in that age as breathing — when with the common people has it not been?* — J. M. Robertson says that "no sequence of vileness nor incompetence in the emperors, no impatience of the insecurity set up

---

* At the moment of writing this, John F. Kennedy and his aides are working hard to build an "image" of him as a very heroic and wise and able leader. This is for the common American people who, having no royal family, have tended to deify the presidents. Of the presidents in this century the two Roosevelts, Wilson, and J. F. Kennedy have deliberately encouraged this, for political reasons.

131

by the power of the army to make and unmake the autocrat, no experience of the danger of a war of claimants, ever seems to have made Romans dream of a saner and nobler system. Manhood had been brought too low."

The worship of rulers was, of course, a cult in Greece before it passed to Italy. Thucydides reported that the people of Amphipolis offered annual sacrifices to the Spartan general, Brasidas; Plato associated heroes with gods and approved the sentiment of Hesiod that departed heroes were angels on the earth. Aristotle said that divine honors were paid at Athens to Harmodius and Aristogeiton, and he himself dedicated an altar to Plato. Let us observe that F. D. Roosevelt has a "shrine" at Hyde Park, that so incenses Mr. Westbrook Pegler. Sparta had a temple for the worship of Lycurgus; Ptolemy Soter was called Zeus, and his son, God. Ptolemy Philadelphus was worshiped as a deity while still alive. Philip of Macedon and Alexander both thought themselves worthy of divine honors. And so it was, with many others.

The cult passed to Italy, where the senate enrolled some of the Caesars among the gods. Sacrifices and vows were offered to Augustus in the Forum and in Egypt, Asia Minor and elsewhere; and temples were built to him in Pergamum and Nicomedia. Honored as Zeus, Olympia called him Savior of the Greeks and of the world; and Ovid spoke of him as being most merciful of all the gods, and of him and Livia and Tiberius as three divinities. Of the emperors, Caligula and Domitian took the adoration most seriously, the one trying to force his statue on the Jews, the other undertaking repressive measures against the Christians.

We all know that infallible wisdom and miraculous achievements were ascribed to Stalin. A huge constellation of miracles enshrined the name of Augustus. It was believed by the common people that as a child he was carried away from his cradle by invisible hands to a lofty tower, where he was found with his face turned to the rising sun. Eagles brought food to him. When a stranger tried to sleep in his bed, he was dragged away by an unseen hand. And when Augustus died, an image of him was seen to rise from the flames of the pyre and ascend in blinding glory to heaven.

How seriously did the emperors accept the homage? Did they

exploit it merely for political ends? Vespasian jested, of course, on his death bed, saying drily, "I think I am becoming a god." But Caligula took his divinity so seriously that he substituted an image of his head for that of Jupiter on many of the statues. Severus scoffed at the language of adoration, but Heliogabalus did his best to unite all forms of religion in a worship of himself. But whether the emperors took the worship seriously or not, the common people did, and most of them still do, in Communism and out of it. The image of the emperor was a recognized refuge for the slave and the oppressed, and the most trivial disrespect to it was a capital crime. It is said that under Tiberius slaves and criminals held in their hands an image of the emperor while with impunity heaping imprecations and curses upon their judges. When a drunkard accidentally touched a ring, bearing the emperor's image, against a profane object, he was immediately denounced as a spy; and another man, who sold an image, was charged with high treason. Indeed, it was a capital offense to undress in the presence of a statue of Augustus, or to enter a brothel with a coin bearing his image. It is recorded that a woman was executed for disrobing before a statue of Domitian.

We turn back for a moment to Robertson's statement, that manhood had been brought too low. The elevation of mortal man to godhood has invariably led to social corruption. The pages of Suetonius are a witness to this — to the cruelties and lusts and moral chaos which steadily paralyzed an empire in which the rulers were gods. If history is any record to go by, the Hitlers and Stalins and Titos, if left unmolested in their autocratic power, must lead their people to the same social disintegration. Ruler worship is largely a displaced father-homage; like Caesar's wife, it must remain above reproach, or in any case its spurious virtues and its deceptions must be hidden from the eyes of its idolaters.

* * *

Let us now look at another aspect of the matter that seems to me to have special significance. The Jews in the time of Augustus had one god, other peoples had many gods; but the deity of the Jews had become lost in remote space. In an earlier time there had been precious intimacy between Yahweh and his people; but Abraham's god had been anthropomorphic, and the Israelites of a later time in an

133

effort to obliterate the offensive anthropomorphisms had steadily elevated Yahweh to a magnificent transcendence, until in effect they lost him. How remote he became we can discover in the pages of Philo.

Now it is an obvious truth that God for the common people must be personal, intimate, and close to their lives and problems. The God of Philo may be a magnificent conception, but he was not the kind of deity who could fill the souls and fire the moral emotions of ordinary folk. It may be true, as the scholars say, that in an effort to restore the intimacy, the Jewish leaders of the centuries just before Philo adopted the Persian angelology, and constituted angels as the intermediaries between God and men. But that was not enough and has never been enough to satisfy the religious emotions of the less intelligent masses.

It was one of the great triumphs of early Christianity, and one of its most potent appeals, that it brought God down to earth again, to manifest his presence in his son. This simple stroke of genius, springing from the yearnings and the needs of the common people, gave Christians an enormous advantage over their competitors.

What was the attitude of the Empire, with its worship of men, toward the Christians? I shall let a few of the ablest scholars state it. Tucker says of the Christian that he took no interest at all in the affairs of the empire but talked of another king and his imminent coming, and of a greater kingdom. "He held what appeared to be secret meetings, although the empire rigidly suppressed all secret societies. He weakened the martial spirit of the soldier. He divided families. . . . He was a socialist leveller. He threatened with ruin the trades connected with the established worship. . . . He not only stood aloof from the religious observances of the state and the household, but treated them with contempt or abhorrence."

As a consequence, says Walker, "Christian refusal to render the worship seemed treasonable, and was the great occasion of the martyrdoms." Again, then, we have a striking parallel, for in the lands controlled by the Kremlin is the largest body of martyrs known to history. Halliday says that a "practical difficulty arose from the Christian refusal to conform to the ritual of the worship of the emperor and Rome, with which all other peoples, except the specially exempted Jews, were perfectly willing to comply."*

No attempt, says Enslin, to force emperor worship upon Judea was ever made, "save perhaps by the mad Caligula — and that attempt was speedily given up after its dismal failure." In deference to the Jews, coins were minted for them with a simple and inoffensive superscription, without the emperor's head. The Christians, says Glover, were the only people in the empire except the Jews who "openly denounced the folly of worshiping and deifying the emperor." The denunciation took violent form in the book which is today called "Revelation," with its frenzied and furious hatred. As the Christians grew in number, they became bolder and more determined, with the result of persecutions and suppressions from the middle of the third century to the triumph of the Church under Constantine. Then the Christians themselves became the persecutors and suppressors.

* * *

It has been said that there are ten thousand printed definitions of religion. There must be as many of God. But whatever God is or is not, this fact is plain, that again he has become lost as physics has expanded our knowledge of the universe to incalculable light-years. The philosopher may have a concept that comforts and sustains him, or the scientist; but the common people do not have. A greater and greater number question whether there is any God at all — any father-image idealized to divinity. They now live in a scientific age of materialism, and though the more enlightened and thoughtful person may get along fairly well, the mass of the people, ineducable and poorly trained, still need to believe in and be guided by a wise and indulgent father-symbol.

Of the Christian sects I should imagine that the Roman Catholic does most to fill that need. This is obviously so because it has a more satisfying ritual and a high ecclesiastical figure who can speak for

---

* The peculiar deference and homage to father and father-symbol in Jews and Christians, which was so superficial in Greeks and Romans, has never, so far as I know, been the subject of an essay; nor do I know of any book that tries to relate this fact to the fantastic increase in juvenile delinquency and crime.

God ex cathedra to the people. But it is well known that even this church is troubled by defections from its ranks, even in its traditional Latin strongholds, and by political threats to its supra-state security. As for the troubles and soul-searching in the other sects, these appear in the journals and the convocations.

We have a western world that is much like the Roman world in the time of Hadrian. History is coming full cycle on us and again we have the worldliness, corruption in high places, crumbling of institutions including that of marriage, detachment from standards and values formerly thought to be necessary to the social order, cynical political opportunism, obsession with material things, and a confusion in religion that reminds one of that in the first Christian centuries. I do not say that we are going to collapse and disappear like the Roman empire, though there are authorities who think this nation has passed its prime.

It seems to be a fact of the present that a Father-God concept is necessary for the spiritual nourishment and health of the common people, and that this concept has become obscured if not lost. If the theologians cannot restore it, the politicians in some manner will. That is exactly what they have been doing. I have been saying in print for a long time that Communism must be viewed, not as a political or economic order, but as a religious order, if we are to understand the emotional appeal it makes to the millions. For its appeal is not primarly a chicken in every icebox and two cars in every garage. Its appeal is to be found in managers who are represented as semi-divine and able to feed the human hungers, and it is to be observed in the cold war that American leaders are offering more and more of the things that children feel they have a right to expect from their fathers, human and divine.

How pointless it is, then, to look on Communsm as atheism, or to imagine that we can contain it with dollars! Millions of people the world over had looked toward Stalin as the common people of the Empire looked toward Augustus. Nobody has suggested that Harry Truman is more than a fallible and mortal man from Missouri. F. D. Roosevelt was one of the gods. For millions inside his country and beyond it he became a symbol, as the Caesars did; and so it was that hysteria swept the nation on his death and rivers of tears were shed over half the world. The hysteria even of many news commentators is fresh in memory, and the choked voices of presumably self-possessed men, occupying high positions. We cannot defeat, we can only copy, Communism by establishing a god in the White House, even if other Roosevelts were to appear. We cannot fight emperor worship with emperor worship, unless we are prepared to descend to the moral level of the Empire under Diocletian. Nor can we, in my opinion, successfully oppose Communism with Marshall and Truman plans, armaments, and propaganda. We can imitate it or rise above it.*

To rise above it, as far as the masses are concerned, we must have a spiritual renascence that will bring God down from his remoteness and again establish his goodness in the souls of men. This is a task for Christian leaders, but they seem to be bankrupt of ideas and ideals. They are so lost in a wilderness of feuds and factions, casuistries and dogmas aand doctrines, that it seems idle to look to them for more than they offer now. No doubt we shall continue the struggle at the low level of materialism with dollars and weapons; and if another war comes we shall find that we lost the Republic when the common people lost God.

*   *   *

In still another way it seems to me that we are a deluded, naive, wishful-thinking, and blundering people. I mean that instead of trying to understand the Communist and why he is a Communist and what it is that he doesn't have and wants we meet him with suspicion, ignorance, denunciation, and jail. We assume that he is in the pay of evil. Well, remember — the scholars are unanimous in this — that the early Christians, struggling against a materialistic Empire, deceived, lied, and deliberately forged documents in an effort to win their case against the enemy. Let us have, briefly, a few statements bearing on this.

"It will scarcely be credited," says Edersheim, a Christian Jew, "how general the falsification of signatures and documents had become." Lecky observes that there was a "deliberate and apparently perfectly unscrupulous forgery of a whole literature, destined to fur-

---

* We are imitating it in welfare states and new frontiers.

137

ther the propagation either of Christianity as a whole or of some particular class of tenets. . . . The Fathers laid down as a distinct proposition that pious frauds were justifiable and even laudable." One of the Fathers, Chrysostom, said, "Great is the force of deceit provided it is not excited by a treacherous intention."

With such amazing statements in mind, Cardinal Newman wrote: "The Greek Fathers thought that, when there was a justa causa, an untruth need not be a lie." It all led, says Draper, "to a want of fair dealing and truthfulness almost incredible to us; thus Eusebius naively avows that in his history he shall omit whatever might tend to the discredit of the Church, and magnify whatever might conduce to her glory." The historian Mosheim says, "It was an act of virtue to deceive and lie, when by that means the interest of religion might be promoted."

Does that throw any light on Communism for you? "It was admitted and avowed," wrote Dean Milman, "that to deceive into Christianity was so valuable a service as to hallow deceit itself." Isn't that the way the Communist leaders look at it? As Professor Tyndall says, "The end being held to justify the means, there is no lack of manufactured testimony." Streeter reminds us that "accuracy and veracity were virtues not widely practiced in the Ancient World — they would be thought quixotic in dealing with political or theological adversaries." We are off the track if we suppose this is peculiar to the ancient world; it is to be found in the character of fanatics of all times. Whether the Communists adopted the methods and practices of the Christians, I don't know. I prefer to think that they merely reached down into their fanatical will to win and found them there.

Those are only a few statements from the many in my notes but they are enough to establish the deadly parallel. The end justifies the means. . . . An untruth need not be a lie in a worthy cause. . . . Pious frauds are laudable. . . . Great is the force of deceit. . . . It is an act of virtue to lie if the cause is promoted — and over that simple axiom of the fanatic what a colossal fool the Western world has made of itself! For it has been unwilling to believe that the Communists are deliberate liars. Roosevelt seems to have believed everything Stalin said, and so we are where we are now.

The Communists hold, and many of them in all sincerity, that the means does indeed justify the end; for as fanatics they believe, as the early Christians believed, in the rightness of their cause. It has always been easy for men, even for the noblest, when convinced of their rightness, to employ the Devil's methods to promote their cause. In looking at Communists it is therefore necessary to understand that fanatics can blind themselves to truths and facts, and distort and pervert in their favor anything that can serve them. It does not follow that they are evil men, unless you are ready to argue that all the saintly ones have been evil. They are merely deluded and fanatical. To say that the sincere and intellectual Communist is vicious would be as silly as to say that St. Paul and Luke and Matthew, or Origen and Clement and Eusebius, were vicious. The Christians believed, as the Communists believe, that the end jutifies the means.

In the magazine *Life* there has recently been an article called "The Making of a Spy." It is about Harry Gold, the small, fat, introverted "lonely outcast" who is to be tried. This man grew up with a morbid sense of being useless and unwanted; he had an intense desire for approval and social fellowship. His unhappy childhood may not justify his treason. It does explain it. What he needed was education*; what he got was chemistry, which is not education at all. It is a pity that we send to jail these uneducated simpletons whose chief fault is their failure to understand human nature and human motives, including their own. If our public school system educated instead of trained, this man would never have betrayed his country. He would have come to terms with his father or his lack of a father.

I have had close friends who were Communists and all of them are very neurotic and unhappy persons.** I have known other Com-

---

* "The ultimate end of education," says Mortimer Adler, "is not just to learn to be an engineer, a lawyer, a doctor, or a scientist. These are skills . . . but knowledge of any one particular subject is not necessarily evidence of an educated man. Education is the sum total of one's experience, and the purpose of higher education is to widen our experience. . . . Most people have only begun their education when they finish school. . . ."
** In my Testament of Man series of novels I call them orphans — that is, children whose parents failed them in early years when they needed a sheltering and protective love.

munists, including college teachers, and in a way all of them are Harry Golds. The Communist intellectual, as I have observed him, if he is not a cynical opportunist, is an evasive emotionally immature idealist, full to his gullet with loneliness, impractical idealism, wishful thinking, and impatience with the existing order. He really believes — and this, born of ignorance, is his fatal weakness and his vice — that if *he* were in a position of power, entrusted with the greatest happiness of the greatest number, he would be wise, able and incorruptible. He scornfully dismisses Lord Acton's famous statement that power corrupts, and absolute power corrupts absolutely. His blind self-love, his narcissistic self-indulgence, and his fanatical talent for converting truth into error in the service of his ends, are possibly the worst that can be said about him. His motives are acceptable if you will grant his major premise. His premise is that persons like him can be, in positions of great power, benevolent and uncorrupted rulers. He is blind to the fact that the best of *that* lot, Marcus Aurelius, has some dreadful blots on his record. His motives are good if you assume that most people are on the side of what is good and right, but only deluded people, ignorant of the past and of themselves, can make such an assumption.

In this great struggle to preserve the little that has been won of freedom and truth the emotional and intellectual illiterates don't count. They are the dumb who follow the blind. The ones to look at sharply are the genuine intellectuals — the persons of really superior quality who believe that Communism, or any form of Socialism or Statism, is the answer to the world's economic and social ills. They are all of them profoundly uneducated people. A few of them, like Koestler, educate themselves and come to their senses, crying mea culpa; but most of them become fixed and lost in their infantile obsession, and our failure to understand them only hastens their flight into martyrdom.

And so, it seems to me, it comes down to this, that the intellectual Communist in this country is largely a product of our inadequate system of public education, which stresses data rather than motives and forces, and of the spiritual vacuum in the Christian churches. These intellectuals are, without being aware of it, godless but god-seeking — fatherless and father-seeking, and emotionally immature; and so, unable to find the inner affirmations and moral certitude which Otto Rank gives as the principal characteristic of great men — that is, unable to give up God and accept an enlightened conscience as one rule to live by they turn to the man-god, the god-man, the father-symbol and pledge to him their loyalty and sometimes their soul. It is a historic fact that many turned in that way to Roosevelt — many to Hitler and many to Stalin. This failure to see that they haven't grown up, emotionally, and come to terms with father and Father is the simple explanation of all the Alger Hisses.

All of us, heaven knows, are ignorant and in some measure evasive and self-deceived. Being so, it is well to keep in mind the profound observation of one who looked more unerringly than most into the contradictory tangle of human motive and yearning. "Unless we allow," says Frazer, "for this innate capacity of the human mind to entertain contradictory beliefs at the same time, we shall in vain attempt to understand the history of thought in general and of religion in particular." That innate capacity is dominant in the soul of the dedicated Communist, as it was in so many of the Christian leaders, and explains why a man who is basically good and worthy can stoop to the most appalling forms of deceit and betrayal.

Portrait of Towser

One look at Towser and you would have known that there was something special in his background. It was not his mother; she was a long-haired collie who had the humility and abashed look of a thing that couldn't figure out why she was allowed to live. But she was a devoted mother to a basketful of pups, and she minded her business and earned her board, which is more than can be said of her son. Her name was Kitty. In her fifth year she took on a male badger in a fight to the death and was buried at the mouth of the hole where she died.

Towser's father was a big handsome nomad, half mastiff and half German shepherd. He was first called Bob but Marco Polo later because he would never stay home. Bob was a pooch dedicated to earnestness; his major interests were females and death of his enemies. When coyotes saw him, they vanished over the horizon. If set on cattle, Bob leapt like a cougar to a pair of haunches and fixed his teeth in flesh, and there he rode, braced and firm, until the terrified beast swept him off by dashing into a thicket. Bob was away from home most of the time. He had a sleepless interest in females and a warrior's heart and he was forever on the go. After three or four nights of wooing and warfare, he would come in, usually wounded and always exhausted, and lie around in the shade, his chin on his paws and his eyes yellow with evil. He killed so many of the neighbors' dogs in his wanderings that someone shot him and tossed his carcass into Snake River.

Those were Towser's parents, and inasmuch as both suffered violent death, it is not strange that their son became so scarred and amputated. I don't know how many times he narrowly missed his end. As a half-grown pup he would seize a cow's long tail and allow himself to be kicked and dragged while he flung his head from side to side as though to tear the tail out, and growled furiously in his throat. He fell into an old well and must have swum around for hours before I found him, almost dead and very soggy and chilled and very grateful for being pulled out. Such things in his life were only minor misfortunes. And so were porcupines. Now any dog with the sense God gives dogs will tackle these deadly creatures once but never twice. Tower could never get enough of them. I was patient with him the first time; with tweezers and pliers I pulled most of the quills out of nose, tongue, and jaws. Some always break off or have been broken off and must be left to work their slow way through flesh or bone. Towser after the operation was so embarrassingly chastened and grateful that I thought the experience would teach him that he was not the master of all things; but within the month he came skulking in, his tail like a cane between his legs and quills like tiny spears of ivory in his lips and gums and over his whole face. Not all the quills from his first experience had yet worked their way out; he had festers and pus cysts and sores inside his mouth. But even though he must have suffered a great deal of pain, he never tried to break away from me and say to hell with it, let them stay there. It was a painstaking and tiresome and ugly chore. If the pain became too acute, the most Towser would do was to give off a little whimper and look with his wonderfully eloquent eyes into mine, as if to ask whether I didn't have better tools or gentler hands.

After enough experiences to teach a dozen dogs not to be fools, Towser would still attack a porcupine. I guess there was just too much of his old man in him. If he wanted to attack but couldn't make up his mind, he would howl with the most heartbreaking in-decision, his eyes begging you to encourage him. He would actually sink back to his hams and wail for an hour; and if the porcupine went skulking away, Towser would follow to keep it in sight, and then sit again and howl. If you sharply rebuked him, he would slink off, his tail dragging the earth, his eyes imploring you to be reason-able; but after a few moments he would race pellmell this way and that, as though to get his blood up and excite his courage, or yours; and he would dash past you in headlong rushes, or twenty yards away he would suddenly drop his chest and chin to the earth and look at you, his tail wagging and begging your assent. But, as I say, all these things were only his minor misfortunes. The tour de force of his life, the epic of his courage, the marvels of his stamina, all came from his relations with a mowing machine.

It had been a habit with him even as a pup to fall into delirious yapping when a team of horses was hitched to anything. He had learned, I suppose, that when a team was hitched it meant a journey and he loved journeys. At first I though he was halfwitted, but I think now that he had merely become part of American speed and dash. He simply went mad or in any case acted completely manic when the team began to move; he would then rush to their heads, barking furiously and falling over himself; and then dive under the wagon and get knocked silly by a wheel and come out yelping with consternation; and at last dash off full speed to right or left as though in pursuit of phantom hares. His frenzies seemed to be determined by the volume of noise around him. If it was a wagon moving off, his dogfoolery was only a kind of violent enthusiasm; but if it was a clattering machine, a gasoline motor, or anything that howled and shrieked, Towser became an uncontrollable lunatic and hurled him-self through more absurdities in an hour than most dogs know in a lifetime.

It was in his second year, when he was a fullgrown handsome bachelor, that he jumped blindly into his first disaster. I was mowing alfalfa at the time. Agog with lunacy and as tireless as a waterfall or a windmill, Towser raced and somersaulted round and round the field, in one moment in wild pursuit of a cottontail, in the next after the shadow of a hawk while howling his head off. Now and then he would come dashing up to me, through the standing or the new-mown hay, his eyes asking for a word of praise; and if I said, "Eat em up, Towser old boy! Go get em!" he would shriek with renewed furies and lose all sense of direction in his mad burst of speed. I could mark his course by the undulating path in the hay. I tried always to keep a close eye on him, knowing well that daily intercourse with so-called civilized beings had stripped him of most of his dog sense. But all my watchfulness got Towser nothing. Suddenly, in the deepest hay, I saw him streaking toward me at full speed. I shouted warnings but he was after a rabbit, the creature leaping into sight and disappearing like a thing of rubber. Towser was roaring his lungs out when he struck the knife and with a yelp of astonishment he vanished in a cloud of hay. Don't ask me why I didn't stop the team: it all happened in an instant, and besides, I was shouting at him and I thought he would stop.

Hours later when he did not come to supper or answer to his name, I searched for him and found him hiding in a thicket. He wagged his tail at me but refused to budge. He looked very chastened and foolish. Crawling into the thicket, I examined him and found that the knife had half-severed his right hind leg, far up in the ham. I though he was hamstrung. Carrying him to the house, I told myself that this dog's days of clowning were over. Because a dog is his own best doctor I did nothing for him; and week after week he lay by the house, licking his wound, or wagging his tail and looking sad and sorry when I approached him. After the wound healed, he began to move around, with the injured leg drawn up until it lay forward along his belly. He learned to run on three legs, swinging his tail to keep his balance. His love of life returned.

A year later, as suddenly as before, he struck the knife again. Again he went into hiding and I had to go looking for him. This time he lost his left hind foot. As before, he lay for weeks, licking the bone, but this time it seemed that his spirit had been completely crushed. To my words of cheer and encouragement he would not even wag his tail or look at me. In despair and disguest or both he went on a hunger strike and I thought he would starve to death. Many an hour I sat by him and talked to him and rubbed a palm over his short thick hair. I told him he would be all right but I

145

didn't see how he ever could be, for he was in a hell of a predicament, with part of his left leg gone and his right leg atrophied against his belly. When at last he moved, he had to crawl, dragging his hind quarters as if his back had been broken. Not yet aware that he had an unconquerable soul, I thought I ought to shoot him; and one day I did come with a gun but I saw something in his eyes and I put it away. I told myself I would wait a while, to see what he would do and what he could do. What he did the reader may not believe, but I am not exaggerating at all; and it is almost an understatement when I say that what Towser did seems to me to be one of the most remarkable and heart-warming achievements I have known or read about.

At first he tried to hobble along on the left stub. The bone became raw and bled, and Towser became depressed. For a week he went into brooding retirement. He simply crawled back under a big serviceberry bush in a grove of aspens, as though to be alone and think about his problem; but after a week he came out, and for a month thereafter when life called to him in its glory and hungers, he would bark his head off. But barking was not enough; the time came when he again tried to run, and his stiff leg, lying up against his belly, would shuttle back and forth like a piston but never touch the earth. Towser would again hide and lick the raw bone, and again try, and each time he ran a little farther than he ran the time before. One day, as though done with brooding, he went to a plowed field where the earth was soft and smoothly harrowed, as though to experiment — there could be no other word for it. Day after day he worked alone and with infinite patience out in that field; and incredible as it may seem, little by little he limbered the half-atrophied and paralyzed muscles of his right leg; little by little he straightened it and brought in down and put it to use.

He then went on three legs, putting the footless one down only in snow or on soft earth. But he used his tail. He used it so much to balance himself that it became as hard and muscular as the tail of a beaver. While growing into old age — at last he had no teeth and he was halfblind — he seemed to become more active than formerly, as though he had to make up for all the months he had lost. For danger, his contempt became stronger; for nonsense, his relish more insatiable, until all who saw him were amazed by what he did.

When feeling the zest and drive that had always been so strong in him (perhaps from his father), he decided in his later years that he had to have something in his mouth. If you paid attention to him when he challenged you to a bit of playfulness, he would then dash off in his wild reckless way and at once seize anything in his path — a piece of stovewood, or of iron; or, if these were not in sight, a feather or a straw would do. But something he had to have and he would race around yelping insanely till he found it. If you played with him, he would then astonish you with his freakish conduct. After dashing roundabout you three or four times, his tail thrust straight up like a cane, his footless leg thrusting up and down but never touching the earth, he would unexpectedly wail like a dog in pain and anguish, as though you had kicked him; but if you took him too seriously, he would stop abruptly and look at you, as though wondering about your sense of humor. Then he would be off, and at the moment when you were certain that he had gone for good he would come pellmell toward you from an unexpected direction, carrying in his mouth a half dozen long rooster feathers, or possibly a stick six feet long. He would drop what he had and look at you and bark and wag his tail, his eyes all the while studying your face; and as likely as not, in his efforts to astonish or delight you, he would dash blindly away and strike a tree and almost knock himself out.

If you started off with a team, he would get a stick or a feather in his mouth and race off ahead of you; and returning, he would actually dash under the wagon between front and hind wheels or between the front and hind legs of the team. If struck by a wheel or a hoof, he would go off yelping as if all his bones were broken; but if, deceived, you took him too seriously, he would cringe and look abashed and ashamed, like one who had carried his nonsense too far. But if you grinned and said atta boy, he would redouble his energy, as if to convince you that getting knocked end over end was all a part of his plan. He would dig for an hour or two in the hole of a badger where he knew no badger had been for months, all the while yelping like mad.

But none of his capers when young or old was as amazing as his behavior toward a gasoline engine. When I got ready to saw stovewood, he knew it at once, and announced with frenzied moans and gurglings, with violent shiverings and quakings, that another crisis in his life had come. His desire seemed to be — but I suppose really was not — to have his jaws torn apart or his neck broken. What he did was to put his open mouth to either the belt or the flywheel and then moan and roar for all he was worth, with flesh frying and blood running. For me it was terribly upsetting to watch him, and I never figured out why he did it: before he lost his teeth, I thought possibly he had an aching tooth and found relief in abrading the gum on speeding iron or canvas. But after all his teeth were gone, he was as bent on it. If I did not drive him away, in a few minutes he was lacerated and bloody from his snout to his ears. If I allowed him to satiate his strange delirious lust, he would exhaust himself in a blood-and-pain orgy and then go away and sleep. If with angry words I drove him from the belt and wheel, he would lie on his belly and look at me, and his eyes said plainly that there was no reason or tolerance in me.

Some of my friends, including a bald professor who fetched along a ridiculous house poodle, watched Towser at the wheel and belt; and when astonishment allowed them to speak, they tried to explain him. One thought his flirting with death and his wanton self-punishment marked him as a halfwit among dogs. Another thought that possibly he suffered from an inferiority complex or sexual impotence! But I looked at the life and fun and humor in the large eloquent eyes and thought of his remarkable courage in times gone. I don't know what it was in this dog with the short yellow hair and the stiff tail but I suspect that my friends missed it. I suspect that his lunacies were less canine than human.

The Failure of Public Education

in a Democracy

When your president asked for the nature of my talk this evening, I told him it would be the failure of public education in a
democracy, I think possibly that is a bad title. To speak of the failure of education is to imply that it tried and failed, whereas the fact
is that it never had a chance to begin with. Democracy and education
occupy separate worlds, and are as allergic to one another as fire and
water. One must wonder what Thomas Jefferson and his zealous
compeers had in mind when they envisaged a brilliant future for
education in a democracy. It may be that these two words had for
them a meaning different from what they have for me, so my first
task is one of definition.

The dictionary says a democracy is a form of government by
the people — a government in which the supreme power is retained
by the people and exercised through their representatives. In the
popular mind democracy seems to mean equal rights and opportuni-
ties, and, for many, equality of intelligence. Failure to understand

* A talk given to the Pacific Northwest Library Association at Sun Valley,
September 23, 1960; and published in its journal, January, 1961.

it has led to the common assumption that one person is as good as another. It surely is obvious to thoughtful persons that to be successful a democracy would need a far greater degree of enlightenment in its citizens than any other form of government, for otherwise it would be only a travesty on itself. That democracy in this country is a travesty on itself is the theme of many books in the libraries which you ladies and gentlemen supervise. There are those, for instance, which have exposed the fantastic power and scope of the criminal underworld, controlled by the Mafia, and doing an annual business of forty billion dollars. It seems unlikely that anyone would argue that an educated people not only would suffer such an appalling condition but be indulgent toward it.

The weakness, possibly fatal, in a democracy is that it allows a bare majority (which may be and often is the least intelligent part of the population) to choose the leaders. This will be so as long as most of those who seek public office are willing to appeal to and flatter stupidity and the baser passions. This weakness works both ways: while the office-seeker is surrendering to the less worthy traits in the electorate, he descends to a level below that which he would normally occupy, and at the same time traduces the people by refusing to disturb their ignorance and prejudice.

If we had an educated electorate, the matter would be otherwise. The dictionary gives three or four definitions of education: the acquisition of knowledge, skill, or the development of character through study; the sum of the qualities acquired through instruction and social training; and pedagogics. Surely one of the major ironies in the educational system of this country is in the title given to that department in which is to be found the least education. For the name of that department is the Department of Education. I never think of educators, in this sense, without recalling an embarrassing experience. It happened when Robert M. Hutchins, the wonder-boy from Yale, who became president of the University of Chicago, spoke in the summer of 1935 to the faculties of the University of Iowa. On concluding his talk he asked if there were any questions. On my left there stood up a small redfaced, completely bald man who stammered a bit but at last got out a question. He stood almost behind Hutchins and about thirty feet back. I can never forget how Hutchins slowly turned his handsome arrogant face until he had a full view of the little man; or the tone of his voice when he said, "Are you a member of the Department of Education?" With obvious pride the little man said he was. With arrogance so cold it was chilling Hutchins said, "I thought so," and dismissed him.

In a few minutes I will try to define education for what it means to me. First, let us look briefly at the picture before us. My thesis is that if our public school system educated, we could not have so many of the phenomena which confront us today. We could not have such incredible vulgarity and dishonesty in much of our advertising. We could not have such halfwittedness, indeed, such infantilism, in most of the television programs. We could not have the level of reading taste that is displayed on the thousands of magazine and reprint stands. We could not tolerate frauds who become national idols — the late Wilhelm Van Loon, as an instance, who was built by his publisher into the image of a brilliant historian and biographer, and who, with nationwide approval from both readers and reviewers, could publish such words as these about the Empress Theodora: "Her body seemed to nestle in the hollow of my arm. She leaned forward and her gentle little breasts touched me. I suddenly understood a thousand years of history. I knew what no mere scholar could ever find out."

A New York publisher has said, "One lie in a Winchell broadcast can sell certain books better than a weekly mention for a year in the *Saturday Review*. Why? Because Winchell is heard and believed by the multitude." No one would dare argue that he is heard and believed by an educated multitude. Joseph Wood Krutch has said that most of the writing in magazines and journals might as well be produced by an electronic brain — and no doubt will be. Another commentator has said that the consumers — young, middle-aged, and elderly — are now regarded as teen-agers by those with merchandise to sell. Quote: "a by-product of this cultural saturnalia dedicated to adolescence is the periodic attack made on intellectuals by mobs of know-nothings." As Franz Schoenberner says in *You Still Have Your Head*, the word *intellectual* is used in this country in a derisive sense, like egghead, highbrow, and other synonyms. Such derisive terms, he says, have no equivalents in European languages.

151

I quote: "The young American nation had been conceived, created, and governed for several decades by an intellectual aristocracy of the highest order. Like all uncommon men, the members of this only true nobility have been often attacked and abused . . . Superior intelligence, great learning, and a well-rounded education in arts and letters were still to be respected and admired — grudgingly perhaps at times, but they certainly could not be ridiculed, because their absolute value was accepted even by the most primitive. The writer has often wondered when and why the turning of the tide began — the total change in America's mental and psychological attitude toward its intelligentsia . . ."

The answer is, when the common people began to come into great power. Now, the magazine *Life*, aimed at the common people and nobody else, sells more copies in a year than the entire paperback book industry. Twenty times as much is spent on sporting equipment as on books. At least one member of a women's book club used to read a book before it was reviewed, but now they have canned reviews, sent out by those who sell books.

Schoenberner again: "Could it be that by a cruel irony the noble experiment of general and universal education inaugurated by Jefferson with the most utopian hopes had somehow miscarried, because the precious privilege of the few, when it was made accessible to everybody, even to those who had never asked for it, necessarily lost its value and fell more and more into disrepect?" Had, he asks, American education "defeated itself by making cheap — in every sense, what in other countries was still the highly prized and priced possession of a cultured minority?" To those questions a number of university presidents said yes, in their commencement addresses last June.

The truth is that only a small percentage of the people can be educated. The great majority can't be, don't want to be, and won't be. They are satisfied with their ignorance and prejudice. Perhaps they are a bit on the order of Miss Ives, the English woman who taught at a school in Paris, when Margaret Case Harriman was there. Miss Ives was so proud of being English that she spoke French with a deliberate English accent. She would take the children outside and waving her English hand would say, *"Regardez let petits oiseaux, mes enfants"* — see all the birdies, children. Her accent could not have been as bad as mine but it was the English quality of it that so infuriated her students that they wanted to break rank and kick all the birdies to death.

In those years when I taught English composition in a university I offered my students this subject for an essay: assume that you may construct yourself from any of the races on earth, taking so much of French, Turk, English, so much of Jew, Indian, Swede. Write me two or three thousand words and tell me what your composition would be. I rarely had a student, and not more than a half-dozen in all the years I taught, who would have changed himself by one drop of blood. When prejudice runs that deep, we may suspect that only those would argue that our public school system is a credit to the money we lavish on it who are quite happy with being what they are.

For training — not education but training — we do have some of the world's best schools — in engineering, medicine, law, and in all the physical sciences. But under the college level most of the training is not worth what it costs. I personally know graduates of the Boise high schools who not only can't write a correct sentence but don't know what a sentence is; who misspell simple commonplace words; and who after twelve years in our public school system, with a B plus average and a diploma, have only the vaguest notion of their duties and obligations as a citizen. It is a tiresome truism to say that they can't read.

The late Albert J. Nock, whom qualified judges would, I think, place among the educated, said in his *Memoirs,* "I do not mean that the great majority are unable to read intelligently; I mean that they are unable to read at all — unable, that is, to carry away from a piece of printed matter anything like a correct idea of its contents." Paul Jordan Smith, at one time a teacher, says in his recent book, "The reason why the unfit are not weeded out is that it would diminish the number of so-called students, which would of course terrify the athletic-minded alumni, contractors who build new dormitories, realtors who sell new additions to the campus — the trustees, the regents, and the State politicians; and those official mouthpieces, the professors of education, who now have state universities by the throat."

153